GHOSTWALK AND OTHER POEMS

Ghostwalk
and Other Poems

JONATHAN MAGONET

Published in 2018 by Kulmus Publishing

ISBN 978-1-988947-02-0

The moral right of the author has been asserted. No part of this publication may be reproduced, stored in a retrieval system or transmitted in any form or by any means, electronic, mechanical, photocopying, recording, scanning or otherwise except under the terms of the Copyright, Designs and Patents Act 1998.

© Jonathan Magonet 5778/2018

Cover illustration © Dorothea Magonet
Cover layout, book design and layout by Marc Michaels
Typeset in Bembo 12pt

For my grandchildren
Ephra and Arava.

Contents

Preface — 9

1. Ghostwalk — 19

2. Miseris Succurrere Disco

Pre-Med
Pathology viva — 20
In the lab — 22
Childbirth — 24
My barber's wife — 25

Medical
Daemon surgeon — 26
On psychiatric grounds — 29
Hospital bed — 31
A man with cancer — 32
Men's surgical — 34
I remember old Lennie — 38
Post-op — 40
In order to drive him mad — 41

Post-op
Penis envy — 44
Treatment — 46
So far so good — 48

3. Germany

Dachau	51
The Guardians of the Law	52
The radical middle	54
Somewhere in Germany	56
Gemeindehaus	58
Old Volks at home	59
Bei Strüdel	60
Ecumen	61
Sermon	62
Bon Voyage	63
The regulation Jew	64
The Nature Theatre of Oklahoma	66
Sick transit	68
Entartete Kunst	69
Render unto Caesar	70
Tea-time at the Park Hotel	71
Kirchentag Leipzig	72
Heidelberg	74

4. Jerusalem

Egged Bus Drivers	75
Uncomfortable in Jerusalem	78
June 1st	80
June 7th	81
Lost and found	82
Give me that old time religion	84
Jerusalem café	86
Jerusalem farewell	88
Arabic class at Ulpan Akiva	90
Language Laboratory	91
Butterflies	92
Ants	93
Dominant	94
Yom Zeh L'yisrael	95
Visitors	96
Visitors Revisited	98
Briefing	102
Report to the committee	104
Again Jerusalem, and again	106
Portraits	108

5. Abroad

I have not yet mastered the beach	110
Hell	112
Art Disco	114
Resort blues	116
Holding the tiger	118
Another moving statue	120
Resort Café	122
Boredom	125
Reps	126
Café Central	128
Cappuccino	130
Dubrovnik	131
Happy hour	132
Bahama mama	134
Roma	136
Novotel	139
Artefacts	140
Moments	142
Street Scene	144
New York interlude	146
Cities	148

6. Portraits

Inflight	150
Broadway and 65th	154
Helena	156
She is grey	158
Arc poetry reading	160
Bal Paré	162
Waiting for Rosi	164
Hanging out with Hesh	166
Shabbat conversations at Sami's	168

7. Musicians

The band	170
The Duo Quiche	174
Hedy's Song	179
The best	180
Talking to the boys in the band	184
Bibo's song	188
Guitar Player	192

8. Japan

A car horn honked	198
Fireflies	200
Rain	203
Cicada	204
A night time stroll	206
The chapel of St Nico	208
Everything changes in Fukuoka	211
In the suburb of Machida	214
Haiku	218

9. Reflections

Jewish writers in concert	220
Waiting	222
Little people	224
For the sake of the poem	226
Once across the sea	228
Exile	230
Visions	231
Kayaking in Alaska	232

10. **Postscript**
    On the way   235

About the Author   236
Acknowledgements   238
Other books by Jonathan Magonet   239
Other books from Kulmus Publishing   242

Jonathan Magonet (right) indulging in some Harmonica Blues.

Preface

I don't know when I started consciously writing poems, or at least rhyming verses. When compiling this collection I came across a notebook in which I had copied out an early would-be 'anthology' ('Poems (and worse) by J.D.Magonet'). Beginning in October 1959 when I was seventeen, the last is dated February 1961. They are a humorous mixture of imagined characters (à la Edward Lear), or comments on aspects of school life, such as chemistry experiments: 'A carbohydrate I once met/refused to hydrolyse....' There was a vein of cynicism:

> By the woolly beard of Pickro
>
> By the banks of Father Thames
>
> There I met a fairy dancing
>
> And the dew was wet around.
>
> Then I asked the fairy dancing
>
> 'Tell me fairy why you dance.'
>
> 'I am dancing for the money!'
>
> And the dew was wet around.

My early passion for detective stories, and an obvious pleasure at broadening my vocabulary, is reflected in the following, the only one of those early pieces that remained in my head.

> At midnight he entered the domed catafalque
>
> And liberally sprinkled the coffin with talc.
>
> He did it because he'd begun to suspect I
>
> Might try to remove the corpus delicti.
>
> But I had avoided this tiresome dilemma
>
> By taking the body at seven pip emma.

Some were a kind of doggerel diary: 'My first day at secretarial school', perhaps the beginning of a journalistic style of writing. Between school and university, Middlesex Hospital Medical School, I had five months working for the society column of the London Evening News, squeezing 'Who, What, When, Where and Why', with a snappy opening and a clever ending, into three short paragraphs. Great training as a writer, and feeding into the desire to pin down and preserve the memory of some experience.

In the same period, I overcame my shyness by joining a Jewish youth club which offered more such events to record, and the chance to publish them in the club magazine, my first potential readership. Such is the nature of youth clubs that regular contributions to the magazine, called simply the 'JM (Junior Membership) Digest', led to becoming editor (a stepping stone to the starry heights of Chairman.) One poem, which I include here for completeness of this historical record, reflects that experience and helps explain why I was probably pre-ordained to spend the last several years as editor of the journal *European Judaism*.

> In Seymour Place, did Kubla Khan
>
> A stately magazine once see,
>
> Where Quink, the sacred river, ran

In fountains measureless to man

Into a hopeless plea.

For twice five sheets of paper ground,

With words and commas were girdled round;

And there were colons stuck there just for thrills,

Which broke up many a sentence into three;

And here were shriek-marks, shaped like iron grills

Enfolding gloomy spots of apathy.

But oh! that tragic plea

Down the white page, to change the Digest cover.

A tearful plea! as hopeless and ungranted

As e'er in magazine was ranted

By ed'tor wailing for his demon-lover.

With apologies to Samuel Taylor Coleridge.

About that time, I came to the conscious awareness that I could 'write', (had I not won the Bethune Short Story prize at Westminster School!) but with it the equally clear realisation that, actually, I had nothing to say. It was my medical school experience that began to provide materials that I felt the need to consider and record, and to do so with a kind of ironic detachment. My first 'grown-up' poems emerged from this period, with quite unexpected success. I sent off three of them, respectively, to *Ambit* ('Childbirth'), the *Transatlantic Review* ('In order to drive him mad') and *Stand* 'Old Volks at home'), and all three were published! Based on that external recognition, I assumed, however naively, that I might actually be, or at least might become, a 'poet'! But I drew the curious conclusion that, this being a given, I no longer needed to be unduly concerned about developing that particular talent! I suspect that the consequent lack of ambition or drive (or imagination, tenacity or courage) accounts for the paucity of my actual output, averaging two poems a year, and the mixed quality of what I produced, as witnessed by this collection.

But in partial defence I need to point to one other area of creativity that became much more central in the same period. I had already enjoyed setting new words to existing songs, either as parodies or to piggyback on the tune for my own compositions for youth club or medical school entertainments.

Jonathan's contribution (far right) to the annual Medical School show, words, music and an athletic performance.

Generations of Jewish youth groupers remember my tribute to a celebrated Israeli bus company with the song 'Egged Bus Drivers' to the tune of the popular Israeli song '*Hava Nagilah*'. But it was during my final years at medical school that I found myself composing songs to my own tunes. I owe much of this to a remarkable man. Leslie Shepard, a folklorist, vedantist and Reichian analyst, was an important figure in the life of Rabbi Lionel Blue, with whom I had begun to work on developing post-war European Jewish communities. Leslie became our spiritual 'guru'. I used to characterise his contribution to our work as 'he kept our metaphysics straight'. He had learnt to play the sitar during his time in India recovering from TB, and helped me acquire my first three guitar chords. Sitting in my hospital room, waiting to be called to attend an emergency as part of my medical training, I started finding music to match the words in my head – and every time I learnt a new chord I set about using it to write a new song. This was an extraordinarily creative period, when the songs simply poured out, and I felt it my task merely to tidy them up. In writing songs, I found my voice, perhaps because I needed melody and rhythm to unlock my imagination. Two of those products, 'Bibo's song' and 'Guitar Player' are in this collection.

I was once invited to perform a couple of my songs at a music master-class. Amongst his comments the teacher asked where I found the music. When I said that it 'sort of comes with the words', he asked, 'has it ever occurred to you that you are a composer?' I felt like Moliere's Bourgeois Gentilhomme who suddenly discovers that he has been speaking 'prose' all his life and never knew it. When I stopped writing songs after about ten years, I never pursued composing, satisfying myself with expanding the small repertoire of melodies I can play on the harmonica. So, I have been blessed by access to two extraordinary gifts, and an alternative universe that I might have inhabited, but never seriously pursued. (An imaginary alternative life in music can be seen in the 'Guitar Player' song.)

But I have also included in this collection two songs inspired by musicians I came to know. Hedy West is rightly acclaimed as perhaps the greatest performer who emerged in the 'folk-revival' of the sixties. I had the privilege of spending time with her during her few years in London, and composed 'Hedy's song' about her, though I don't think I had the courage to sing it for her. When the great cabaret performer and actress Pearl Bailey was in London she did some Bible study with me (by then I had settled for my real 'vocation' as a rabbi and Jewish Bible scholar) and I had the *chutzpah* to sing for her my 'Bibo's song'. She liked it enough to get one of her musicians to write out the music and she sang it on her last night's performance in London at the Talk of the Town. For Pearl, based on stories she told me, another journalism exercise, I wrote 'Talking to the Boys in the Band'.

Having confessed to 'squandered' talents, I am including in the 'Musicians' section some sketches I drew of jazz musicians that I heard in clubs in London, Berlin and New York, in those same early sixties.

My work with Rabbi Lionel Blue took us around Europe and particularly to Germany. This was part of a conviction that, as Jews, we needed to cross the emotional barrier that prevented us visiting that country, the 'land of the murderers'. If we were serious about helping rebuild European Jewish communities, we had to address our own prejudices and work with a new post-war generation. Some of my poems, in the section on 'Germany', reflect much of the early ambivalence about such a venture. But it was in Germany that I found myself engaged in what turned out to be a lifelong commitment to interfaith dialogue with

Christians and Muslims. On a train returning from my first visit to Berlin I realised that I had made the decision to leave medicine to study for the rabbinate. And Germany was where I met my wife Dorothea who designed the cover for this collection and for a *Festschrift* edited by former students to mark my seventieth birthday.

Part of my journey into Jewish studies led me to Israel to start studying Hebrew seriously in the fateful spring of 1967. My last medical activities took place as a volunteer in Hadassah Hospital in Jerusalem during the 'Six Day War', reflected in the poem 'Jerusalem June 1967'. They looked at my medical qualifications, one year of medical and surgical hospital experience in the UK to become registered as a doctor, and put me in the delivery room. So, I spent that war doing episiotomy repairs, and sometimes helping with the wounded. Once I played my guitar and sang some of my songs for the exhausted medical staff. Some of the extraordinary impact of Jerusalem, and the political ambiguities it invokes, can be found in the 'Jerusalem' section of the collection.

Other poems, 'Abroad', emerged from the boredom of seaside holidays and from observations during other journeys. Sketches of people I have encountered appear in 'Portraits'.

When I retired from my post as Principal of the Leo Baeck College, the seminary for training 'progressive' rabbis for the UK and Continental Europe, I decided I wanted to learn a new language. For some reason I opted for Japanese (Chinese seemed too difficult because of the need to master the different tones) and by a series of contacts found myself as a visiting research professor at Seinan Gakuin University, a Baptist founded University in Fukuoka. Their strong theology department was led by Professor Yoichi Kobayashi who had spent time in America and Israel and welcomed a rabbi willing to teach the Hebrew Bible. A one-off visit turned into an annual three-month stay, with the opportunity to learn Japanese and reflect on a very different culture. It even produced a Japanese book containing translations of some of my university lectures, though, sadly, my Japanese is not yet up to reading it! But my time in Japan also gave me the opportunity to stretch my long-neglected fiction skills. I had begun a small collection of 'Netsuke', carved figures formerly used to attach a kind of purse to men's kimonos before western dress became fashionable. Walking daily to the university I found myself writing stories about the imagined life of the figures I had collected, while at the same time reflecting on the Japanese culture I was beginning to experience.[1] An early Japanese language class at the university gave our mixed bag of students the opportunity to write three 'Haiku', which only the arrogance of ignorance allows me to reproduce in the section on Japan.

An unexpected bonus of my time in Japan was the invitation to perform a concert at a music school in Fukuoka of some of my songs, and to accompany the singer and pianist, who teach at and run the school, on my harmonica. Thanks to what has become an annual event at least one early musical talent has had a late flowering. (I am proud to point out that my concerts are always sold out, but with only thirty seats available this is a modest achievement.)

---

[1] *Netsuke Nation: Tales from Another Japan* (Troubador Publishing Ltd, 2013).

Harmonica at the ready from 1964 - 2017.

If I have been somewhat circumspect in the way I regard my poems, it is because so much of my creativity has gone elsewhere in my career – particularly into learning how to 'read' and interpret the extraordinary narratives and poetry of the Hebrew Bible. I am fortunate in having had the opportunity to pass on such skills as I have acquired not only to generations of rabbinic students, but also to Christian theologians and lay people in Germany and Japan.

It has also been my privilege to contribute to the editing of a range of Jewish prayer books, including writing meditative or poetic passages to enhance them. If that adolescent literary creativity has found its expression, it has been mostly in these areas. But from time to time a person, an event or an observation needed to be composed and recorded in the form of a poem, and this collection is an expression of gratitude for a talent that may never have reached fruition, but never quite died.

Perhaps it is also a quiet denial of, or riposte to, the conclusion of the poem that gives this collection its title.

Jonathan Magonet
London, January 2018

Ghostwalk

Feet absurdly float
in frozen rhythm
groping hands remove
intruding snares
ears alone detect
my wary passing.

Should not stumble
tumble over cliffs
blunder into walls
with this technique.

Perhaps if I am skilful
have some luck,
might reach the end
and never once reveal
that I was here.

London March 1967

Miseris succurre disco

PRE-MED

Pathology Viva

1.

Damp-palmed students

in funeral black

await the call

on a corridor bench.

Fervently

we offer up our souls

for a pass,

forgetting that

souls

are no longer

in the syllabus.

2.

They've stopped for tea now,

running an hour late,

grey-haired, stoop-shouldered

inquisitors

behind their specimen pots.

When they, in turn, are potted

we will ask the questions.

3.

They have the advantage

of knowing me.

'You're number 456,

aren't you?'

4.

When it's over

and not too bad

sneak sheepishly

past the curious stares,

somehow

guilty.

London, November 1964

In the lab

1.
Some Rats
that wished to study Man
constructed a maze
in which they performed tricks.
Despite numerous observations
they still could not understand
the reactions of their observers.

2.
The man in the white coat
carries his notes into the lab.
The Rats squeal their recognition.
Till now he does not rely on this
to know who he is.

3.
One of the Rats
a veteran of many tests
began to think he was special
not out of vanity
but because he was chosen so often.
When killed
he merely regretted
the lack of recording devices.

4.
The salivating dog
was more annoyed
at his lack of self-control
than at learning
it was only for a bell.

5.
In order to reduce the variables
we removed the liver, pancreas,
spleen and kidneys.
An external gastric fistula was prepared
and electrodes stimulated
five separate areas
of the decorticate brain.
The results from fifteen rats
were significant
within the statistical parameters.
($p<0.05$)
Naturally we must be guarded
in assessing their significance
in terms of the I.H.B.
(Intact Human Body)

London April 1965

Childbirth

Scrub up

Sterile gown

Episiotomy

Head delivered

Pharyngeal suction

Clamp and cut cord

Ligatures

Uterus contracted

Controlled cord traction

Placenta expelled

Measure blood loss

Placenta and membranes complete

Cord blood taken

Temperature, pulse and pressure

Scrub again

Stitch-trolley

Repair perineum

Feel abdomen

Write up notes

Cup of tea

August 1963 (Ambit 1965 No. 25 p 23)

My barber's wife

My barber's wife died three weeks ago.
He told me awkwardly
fumbling with the scissors
sorry to inject tiresome reality
into our haircut chat.
I mumbled helplessly about 'suddenness'.
'No,' he said,
'she had a breast off three years ago
at your hospital.'

He removed a paper bag from the shelf.
'Bread!
Do my own shopping now.
Better hide it
someone might want a haircut and sandwich!'

We groped through vacant moments:
his daughter
relations who would help
her last days in a ward for incurables.
He watched me in the mirror
with eyes I could not understand,
our teasing familiarity
no preparation
for death.

London September 1965

MEDICAL

Daemon surgeon

    Daemon surgeon
    dressed in green
    white boots
    mask
    hands drip water
    wrestled from theatre plumbing
    notes cockroach in instrument cupboard
    spider hanging from centre light
    at emergency midnight.

    Shrugging into green gown
    knots by sleepy nurse in shapeless white
    plunging neckline
    moment's tingle enticement
    stooped for gloves
    size seven.

    Clutter sound of instruments
    scrubbed charge nurse bellows orders
    clumsy

echoing off plaster walls
screened windows
stainless-steel machines
that boil dead.

Bare black table
rubber soft
rises
tilts
turns
jointed obedience
waits naked the fatted
always fat
sacrifice of organ
limb
unearned
unwanted.

Murmurs from the ante-room
initiation of maimed
correct God's errors
painless rites
refined for modern needs.

Injections

hiss of gas

spun knob

balanced scents of sleep

routine

routine check

part-time priestess still uncertain

all the ampoules entered

bag respiring

meters ticking

snatch off mask

and push the sanctum doors.

Swinging back

all eyes on altar trolley

white-robed body

shaven naked

blushless pink

gift-wrapped appendix

offered up

that he might live.

London February 1966

On Psychiatric Grounds

No one likes to terminate.
They bleed a lot
some nurses won't assist,
and then ...
uneasy scraping life
off the back wall of a womb.

Doctors' safety notes discuss
errant husband
kids at home
pregnant by another
danger to her mental health
the only way ...

She lied about the dates.
among the shredded scraps
placental debris
blood
a tiny, perfect, solitary
foot.

London March 1966

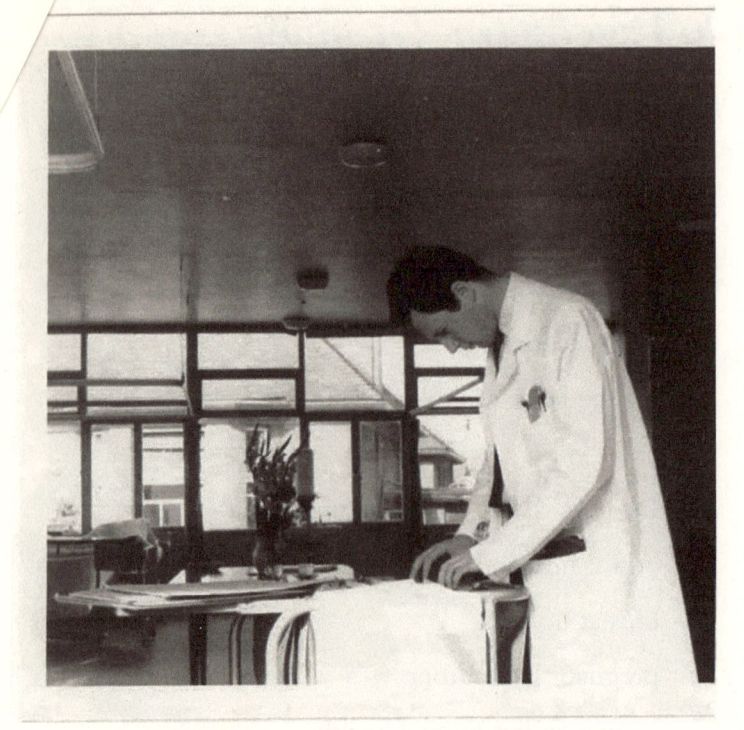

Willesden General Hospital Houseman.

Hospital Bed

The original cot-side

consisted of vertical bars

with a horizontal top-piece.

It was found that this apparatus

though admirably functional

quickly dismantled

easy to clean and store

gave the already confused occupant

of the bed

the quite erroneous impression

of being

imprisoned.

Feb 1967 London

A man with cancer

A man with cancer
swollen belly
rock-hard mass he'd carried half a year
refused all treatment
said he'd cope all right
made Sister most indignant

But sheepish back next week
he sat erect in bed
pursuing you with staring eyes
of anger

Awaiting anaesthetic
hair awry
no glasses
snapped the stubborn self-control
he sobbed aloud:
'This shouldn't be happening
shouldn't happen
to me.'
Until with sleep
the helpless belly search
beyond reprieve.

Returning to the ward

he went quite mad

did handsprings out of bed

ran naked

screamed

'I'm cured!

I have the power!'

Attacked the nurses

warned:

'They're BASTARDS!

Out to KILL YOU!'

Later abject in apology

until the next tirade.

When sedatives had failed

they took him to a mental home.

'There's a gun aimed at my head'

he said

for he was mad

beyond control

and soon would die.

London March 1966

Men's surgical

Bed 1.
Little man,
shy,
with slanted face
and crooked back
who shrank each day in size
within the vastness of his bed
and one day
quiet
cured
just disappeared.

Bed 2.
Half his body useless
second stroke
rasping air through throat tube
speechless
vegetable
near death
who dragged himself
in painful weeks
to walk again
and grunt
and gesture

sudden
unexpected
staggered gamely
stubborn
home.

Bed 3.
Him we pass discreetly
awkward
impotent to act
final hours that linger
into empty days
and weeks
with no excuse of pain
to ease him on his way
who lies
confused
in peace
with sometimes mute reproach
to grind us down.

Bed 4.
Old faithful
groaning as we enter
coughing
pills to keep him breathing

make his heart beat
aid his kidneys
beer and brandy
one leg off
the other rotting
daily prouder of blackened toes
that keep him here in comfort
stalling
till the next reprieve.

Bed 5.
Demented old bloke
'privates' swollen up
and BLOODY tender!
'THEY HAD TO SEND THE FIRE BRIGADE!'
to help him breathe.
No-one at home
neighbours sick of nonsense
await a chronic bed
to lose him in.

Bed 6.
Grouser
pains in tummy
side
sleepless

juggled analgesics
sedatives
placebos
cannot cure the crabby frown
or ancient practised whine.
Smiled just once
when told he'd have his pain
forever.

Bed 7.
Drastic operation
gives him two
or even three years more
if lucky.
Wife
and growing kids
to watch the signs appear
of awesome
slow disintegration
to ask
torment us still:
Why him
so good
so young
so kind
who never hurt …

London June 1966

I remember old Lennie

He was a miserly man in his eighties
brought in as near death
as makes no difference.
But we gave him the drugs
put up a drip, catheter, waited
and over the next few days
almost as if to shame us
he clawed his grim way back.

He lay for months in bed
with his daily catalogue:
'The condition of the bowels is improved today.'
'I'm not really eating as much as I should like.'
and scattered around him
papers, shares, dividends, certificates,
the measure of his life.

He started to walk again
would grab you daily in the corridor
faded, shrunken
with burning eyes

urine bag in hand

'What exactly was the result of the last blood test?'

He found an old people's home

where he didn't have to pay

fixed it through his sad-eyed, broken son.

But as the time came near

he grew more urgent, worried:

'About the bladder

is it a permanent blockage?

Could I do without the tube?

Is this positively final?'

We had to give him one more chance.

'So mean he wants to keep his urine!'

One morning, early, we pulled the catheter out

and watched,

measured through the day

each eager drop he passed

held off the decision, stalled

he might put out a little more …

But in the end, at midnight,

back it went.

He staggered on undefeated

each day walked more

busy with his shares

preparing to move to the home

juggling his opening medicines

but something was different now.

'It's not the natural opening, is it?' he would smile

and now, at last, he knew he'd soon grow old.

London October 1966

Post-Op

Beside the bed

discussing drip

his diet

drugs we'd try

bladder function

bowels

the pressing need to clear his chest.

Hardly time to tell him

he was dying.

London November 1966

In order to drive him mad

In order to drive him mad

put him in a bed

in a ward

in a hospital

and let him know he's ill.

Not how ill

or what illness,

merely suggest it is

very, very grave.

Test blood, urine, sputum, X-Rays

but always be awaiting one more

key result.

Discuss him at the foot of the bed

in whispers

in loud erudition

with worried frown

with anecdotes

with laughter

that he cannot share.

Establish about him an air

of urgency

efficiency

into which, apologetic,

he must intrude

his trivial pain.

Drug him at night

by day

give each injection, pill

its own mystique

and timing

and importance.

Then one day

quite without warning

change it.

Surround him with noise, activity

remove all privacy

make sure at least one patient

in a nearby bed

expires

and let him learn and fear those signs

of awkwardness

embarrassed glance

that mark the next to go.

If all these measures fail

as time goes by

and interest in him

 slides away

suggest he goes back home

relaxes for a while

no overwork or strain

just takes it easy

returns for blood tests now and then

and with a final, hesitant frown

bid him

adieu.

(Transatlantic Review 27 Winter 1967/8 p68/9)

POST-OP

Penis Envy

Since the operation

the plumbing is much improved,

an innocent,

unselfconscious pleasure

regained.

No more the nightly trips,

the woeful trickle

the waiting to begin

uncertain of the end,

the need to blot and mop.

No longer jealous

of those torrents pounding the basin

in the adjacent stall,

of those spouting jets

cataracts

power showers

triumphal gushes,

all that hydrodynamic hyperbole.

Admittedly,
a terminal dribble remains,
but those post-op urgencies
potential embarrassments
trapped on a bus,
somewhere on Finchley Road
no relief available
no salvation in sight
no closet for my water,
seem, mercifully, to be past.
(Thank you God for creating
shopping malls.)
Indeed, with careful liquid intake
up to two hours between passing
are now within my grasp.

So all things considered
it's been a great success.
Let's hope the same can be said
for what still remains to be done.

March 29 2006

Treatment

Still to look forward to

are seven weeks of daily radiation:

(Higher dose,

better localisation

better statistics

than when it was only six.)

Side effects?

Well,

only thirty percent risk impotence.

The irritable bladder

rectal bleeding

lethargy

may improve in time.

Hormonal preparation

may help in the long term

if you don't mind

the hot flushes

and guaranteed impotence.

(Sometimes an erection

is only an erection.)

Maimonides,

that wise old doctor,

taught:

'the cure should not be worse

than the disease itself.'

But with only diet

and a few herbs on offer

what did he know

of prostate specific antigens

of trans-rectal ultrasound and biopsies

of magnetic resonance imaging scans

of computerised tomography scans

or, for that matter,

of Trans Urethral Resection

and post-operative radiotherapy?

Besides,

in his days

who lived long enough

to die of

cancer?

29 March 2006

So far so good

So far so good

but the odds are changing.

'Mild, asymptomatic renal deficiency'

something like that I could cope with,

has a nice ring to it,

so why do they have to call it

'Chronic Kidney Disease',

grades one to five?

So irreversible,

such finality,

not to mention

an unpronounceable acronym.

Of course,

there's the odd skipped heartbeat,

even though that's been around for a while.

I rather liked the word

'ectopic'

but no longer,

documented by a twenty-four hour ECG

threats of potential atrial fibrillation,

seemingly unending lists

of medical and surgical interventions
and increasingly dire scenarios.

All this alongside
the regular measurements
to check
blood cholesterol,
vitamin deficiency
and that mysterious annual decimal figure,
souvenir of a departed prostate.

Add, for the inconvenience,
the frozen shoulder,
relic of a fall in the street
and the computer-induced,
chronic bad posture-related,
stiff-neck
to be pummelled,
stretched,
massaged,
exercised
and occasionally even electrocuted
into submission.

That only leaves,

engagingly innocent

in this hi-tec diagnostic world,

ear wax

somehow thicker

more stubborn now

in one ear.

At least it offers

a symptom,

and low-tec treatment

with oil and a water jet

and that clever little Japanese bamboo scoop.

To complete the inventory

the occasional rash

and one over-productive sinus.

So,

all in all,

coming up to seventy

I'm still marginally ahead

till the next

uninvited

betrayal.

Fukuoka 10.5.2012

Germany Germany Germany

Dachau

Dachau
is a pretty town in summer.
Bright, flowered gardens
line the pleasant, sunshine walk
from bus-stop to Camp.

No smoking in the tidy,
well-planned museum
of photo's, documents.
Thirty pfennigs a programme.
Only thirty thousand died here.

The prison huts are gone.
Artists' memorials
Catholic, Protestant, Jewish
equally-spaced, -sized
bear suitable words of grief,
warning.
The ghosts should be repaired in time
for next year's tourists.

Munich July 1966

The Guardians of the Law
For Peter Levinson

    The guardians of the Law

    are old,

    broken.

    In the house of prayer

    they weep

    the half-truths of their lives.

    The shades of former glory,

    pride,

    intrude no more,

    the light too dim

    for eyes grown weary blind.

    One time

    a ram's horn blew.

    Once, they say,

    a prophet came

    thundered, mocked

    spat his righteous anger.

    But troubled echoes drowned

    in rattle-throated prayers.

The shrunken ghosts
apologise.
They did not choose to live,
the best have gone:
mighty men of wisdom,
gentle rocks of justice.

The guardians of the Law
uncomprehending,
dazed,
repeat the habit tasks
that help them know,
together,
who they are.
And if they do not heed
the pleading of the young
or hide behind their souvenirs of pain,
remember who they were
how stubbornly they clung
and hear with awe the challenge
of their dead sons' sons.

Heidelberg July 1966

The radical middle

The smiling men	The earnest men
no longer need	vaguely dressed
chocolate shirts	in last year's pink
and liquorice boots	see themselves
to whet the appetite	as well-intentioned
The smiling men	The earnest men
are dressed in suits	in sullen shirts
of business grey	and see-through glasses
hunt in middle-aged packs	regret they have
	so little time
	to smile
The smiling man	The earnest man
removes his glasses	is angry
loses the eyelid twitch	incoherent
plausible	forcing them
urgent	to punish them
from a thousand years'	for hurting
rehearsal	them

The smiling man	The earnest man
tense on his seat	of dialectic
cocks his head	protocol
thrashes the innocent air	sits around urgent tables
is not responsible	debating how to start
if old men elect him	the agenda
The smiling men	The earnest men
perspire	do not perspire
recall with pride	despise
the Autobahn	the Autobahn
and wish to burn	and wish to burn
Gunther Grass	Gunther Grass.

Germany   September 1969

Somewhere in Germany

1.

The assistant Burgomaster

a small man

'as a doctor and historian'

stridently urged

the assembled international youth

to build a lasting

CHRISTIAN

brotherly

Peace

PEACE

PEACE!!!

Later discovered

he was not allowed in the Nazi party

because of his reputation

as an abortionist.

2.

The assistant Burgomaster

(who was not allowed in the Nazi party

because of his reputation

as an abortionist)

asked Herr S

how he could allow his blonde daughter

to marry an Italian.

3.

The son of

the assistant Burgomaster

(who had 'a difficult time'

because he was 'never in the party')

has been studying medicine

for seventeen years

without completing the course

in unconscious anticipation

of the second coming.

London January 1971

Gemeindehaus

In the empty new Gemeindehaus
        with the Sauna bath in the basement
not in the room with the ping-pong table
        next to the smart old-people's home
nor in the well-heated offices
        beside the pretty little synagogue
but in the youth group room
        attached to the ultra-modern flats
in a corner on the shiny radiogram
        with a kindergarten on the ground floor
lay unnoticed for two years
        and photos of Israel everywhere
a child's papier-maché mask
        the classroom is closed during the day
its crude, clown face twisted in pain.

Germany March 1967

Old Volks at home

In Volksburg
50,000 citizens
make
Wolfswagens.

The factory
has four horns
and a single large blue eye
that never closes
rarely sees anything.

The town was built by
Adolf the First,
an animal lover,
in the shape of
a beetle.
Despite technical improvements
over the years
(new churches,
cultural centres,
better suspension)
it keeps the same appearance
and the old tendency
when going downhill at speed
to drift to the right.

Germany March 1967 (Stand 9:1 1967 p 62)

Bei Strüdel

At Strüdel's

they keep a pet vulture,

quite small,

trained to swoop down

and eat the remnants off your plate.

Very economical

as pets go.

People feel nervous

but it is quite harmless,

and will never attack a human being

while still alive.

Indeed

they hope to develop this feature

as a way of testing visitors.

Bendorf December 1970

Ecumen

Köln Synagogue

the rabbi

in grey

hands clasped behind

tummy protruding

comfortable

in German.

Köln Synagogue

the priest

in black

hands clasped in front

tummy protruding

comfortable

in English.

Bendorf August 1970

Sermon

Dear friends

Faith of our fathers

Meaning of tragedy

Grapple

Abraham in Sodom

Confrontation with God

Job

(Pause)

Six million

The Berditchev Rebbe

A still, small voice

(Pause)

'Yet still I believe!'

(Pause)

Amen

8.8.65

Bon Voyage

The Israeli Embassy

in Bonn

is a small, square building

painted blue.

Once a year

a man with a beard

inverts it

collects the contents

leaves a receipt

and goes up

to the land.

August 1969

The Regulation Jew

The regulation Jew
for purposes of
Dialogue
Zusammenarbeit
should not be short
or over-plump,
regular features
fluent in at least two languages
left in most opinions
and, preferably,
a guitarist.

Grave, when talking of
The Past
but with the occasional rueful look of
Understanding.
He cannot
Forget or
Forgive
not having
The Right,
 but one must also live for
Today and for
Tomorrow.
(Though nothing that he says
may be considered in any way
Official.) *Germany March 1967*

Breaking the ice at the first Jewish-Christian Bible Week, Bendorf 1969.

The Nature Theatre of Oklahoma

'VOLKSFEST
PATRICK HENRY VILLAGE
HEIDELBERG
TO CEMENT
GERMAN-AMERICAN RELATIONS
GRAND FIREWORK DISPLAY
ON JULY 4.'

                You can go round in circles

                slowly

                on the ponies,

                faster

                on the roller coaster,

                where the lights flash

                and the girls scream,

                fastest

                on the great spinning wheel

                which also takes you

                up and down.

'JULY 3RD IS THE
90TH ANNIVERSARY
OF THE BIRTH OF
FRANZ KAFKA'

> The family stocked up here
>
> last year
>
> on American ice cream
>
> but got tired of it.

'DESPITE GERMANY'S

REVALUTAION OF THE

D-MARK

THE DOLLAR CONTINUED

TO FALL

ON THE FRANKFURT EXCHANGE.

THIS IS A.F.N. FRANKFURT

BROADCASTING

TO YOU

IN STEREO.'

> The man calling
>
> Bingo
>
> Was too pushy
>
> So we left.

Heidelberg July 1973
(European Judaism Vol 8 No. 2 Summer 1974 p.34)

Sick transit

    Among religious games

    which may be accounted

    dangerous

    leapfrog

    comes high on the list,

    not from the risk

    of pushing a brother

    into the ground

    but because

    a zealot

    once sprang so high

    that he soared

    by mistake

    into heaven.

    Trapped

    unwillingly forever

    in the sky

    not only did he lose the game

    but being frightened

    of heights

    he never even enjoyed

    the view.

Entartete Kunst – Degenerate Art

Three million visited the original
on its long tour through the Reich.
Even this anniversary exhibition
has been held over for a month.

We watch the silent footage,
visitors strolling through the original:
stately matrons, well-dressed gentlemen
faces betraying nothing
perhaps on their way
to afternoon coffee and cake.

Is someone filming us,
dressed for a hot summer day
as casual and *entartete*
as the pictures on the walls?
Who will interpret our faces
in fifty years?
in what unlikely exhibition
in what yet inconceivable world?

Berlin May 1992

Render unto Caesar

The Synod of the Brandenburg church
has sent out a questionnaire
to all pastors who had contact with the former DDR
and perforce dealt with the Stasi,
the security arm of the State.

It asks for honest heart-searching,
for repentance,
to be once again at one with God.
Were you asked to name names?
Did you perhaps betray someone
in your dealings?
Confession is good for the soul.

But in such uncertain times
God's love alone may not suffice.
So, give us some names to pass on,
to bring justice to former victims,
absolution to the new State,
security to the Church.

Failure to return the completed form
will, of course, invite investigation,
on earth as it is in heaven.

Berlin, May 1992

Tea-time at the Park Hotel

Tea-time at the Park Hotel.
Two elderly ladies have joined my table
debating the relative discomfort
of the cold chair on the open patio
against the stuffiness behind the glass doors.

It had been my fantasy to celebrate here my fiftieth,
two glamorous ladies on my arm
the promise of pleasures to come.

My two old ladies have opted for the warmth
one complaining, the other grumpy.
The elderly three who replace them are quieter
reminiscing about old times, holidays,
family events.

It is restful in their company
despite the wasp that hovers over my cream-topped slice
of marzipan-sided fruit cake.

God willing, I will join their successors
twenty years from now
by turns querulous or quiet,
but, in my fantasy, only the cream-topped slice
of marzipan-sided fruit cake.

Park Hotel Bremen 4 August 1992

Kirchentag Leipzig

Two single ladies sit at the bar

in the lobby of our old DDR hotel;

two flowers left over from the former regime

make-up harsh in the lobby light,

still awaiting some party official

on his night off.

The red-head

in a tight pink skirt

expressionless

sashays twice to the ladies room

and sashays back.

Her dark-haired neighbour

shares the neutral stare,

not even a friendly nod between them.

Every occasion has its etiquette.

Our fellow conference guests

engrossed in ecumenical gossip

seem not to notice them

called as we are to another profession

equally old.

But how sad not to converse

across this solemn lobby;

compare notes

on why fewer want our services today

or discuss how inflation affects

the wages of sin.

On this, it seems, we agree:

our best transactions

are still conducted in private rooms

where intimacies or confidences are exchanged,

not in public lobbies

of conference hotels.

Even dialogue

for all its many charms

can only go so far.

Leipzig 22.6.97

Heidelberg

Thirty years on

Heidelberg

has lost none of its charm.

Students remain students.

Tourists remain tourists.

Professors remain grey

and lecture

at length

to themselves.

Are they some of my

contemporaries

in seminars

and lengthy lectures

we joked about?

Maybe I alone saw the joke.

Maybe the joke was on me.

Heidelberg Oct 2001

Jerusalem

Egged Bus Drivers
(To the tune of Hava Nagilah)

We are the drivers,

Egged bus drivers,

Who take you everywhere on your stay. (2)

We are the drivers,

We have nine live(r)s

But beware anyone who gets in our way.

You will learn to hate the

Way we take the corners badly

Roaring through the Negev badly

And you would dismiss us gladly,

Yes you would dismiss us gladly,

Though we jest,

We're the best

Drivers in the Holy Land.

France they drive on the right side,

England the left side,

And so we compromise (2)

We are all yiddeleh

Drive down the middle(eh)

And we don't kiddle(eh)

In what we say,

See us overtaking

Blow the horn and pull out blindly

Heaven help the guy behind me.

Hope the cops will never find me,

Hope the cops will never find me,

Though we jest,

We're the best

Drivers in the Holy Land.

Composed in the early sixties.

*Jonathan Magonet atop a very different
mode of transport with equally poor suspension.*

Uncomfortable in Jerusalem

For the time being

I will keep my *kippah* in my pocket

and wear it when appropriate

to study

in *shul*

and on the way there through the streets of Jerusalem

at least on *shabbat*.

For the time being

I will tease the 'reformers'

to whose curious company I sincerely belong

and apologise to the 'orthodox'

whose troubling power I admit with unease.

For the time being

I will continue to feel inadequate

to feel a vocation

to dislike services

to pray each day

and to journey, when the chance arises,

with Christians and Muslims I trust.

For the time being

I will try to teach from experience

to learn from any teacher

to see through what is phoney

and sometimes to fight.

For the time being

I will choose my 'religious' friends

for their love, for their whimsy

and my 'secular' ones

for their faith.

For the time being

as a reasonable Jew

and acculturated European

I will try not to cheat

and so remain

uncomfortable in Jerusalem.

Jerusalem June 1967

June 1st

The calendar maker
awaits only
a date
a result
to declare
the new festival.

A day of joy?
A fast?
Who
and where
to celebrate?

He hesitates –
the calendar is full
the balance almost perfect
so many still to add.

The sightless beg
just one more shade
and with a shrug
he writes.

June 7th

Two stars

darkening rainbow sky

pink-rimmed Jerusalem hills

a cricket

distant gunfire

blood on my white coat.

Hadassah Hospital, Jerusalem, June 1967

Lost and Found

Such, indeed, is the holiness of Jerusalem
that the Post Office auctions if off
at regular intervals
in bulk.

'Holy books'
that by some oversight of divine providence
(and the aforementioned Post Office)
have strayed from their destined path
can be redeemed in anonymous packages
by those with a feeling for the sacred
- or facilities for re-marketing
at a price more suited to their worth.

Scattered among crates
of assorted underwear
of twenty identical parts to an unidentified machine
of shoes and tubes of toothpaste
of sardines, children's games and one coffee tin
of endless clothing
of an incomplete set of Shakespeare in French

of a complete set of something in Polish,
are these jewels of religious wisdom
of perceptive commentary
of refutation and polemic
of saintly dreams
of pious admonitions
- prayers of the holy people
tossed about in the familiar indignity
of yet another temporary exile.

Going for the first time,
going for the second time,
GONE!!

Give me that old time religion

Four abreast we stride the beach

the dawn patrol of the golden agers.

Seventeen minutes briskly

skirting the soft sand

nimbly over the sewage outlet

breathing in the vistas of sky and sea

in measured gasps.

Past the back of the high-rise blocks

the first deckchairs

a sudden nest of children

the glazed intensity of oncoming peers

chugging through our ragged ranks.

The return is leisurely

pausing to enjoy the *hamsin* calm of the sea

pale shades of blue

fading into grey

brushed by the faintest purple haze

a subtle gift of urban fumes

caressing the margin of sea and sky.

Sand brushed off, sandals on

await the womenfolk drifting behind

home to breakfast fritters – unsweetened

coffee – no sugar.

Sabbath day ritual in the Holy Land

counting our blessings of the morning

offering up calories of praise.

Tel Aviv 5.11.90

Jerusalem Café

There aren't enough bag ladies in Jerusalem
that they have to import them
from Brooklyn?

She harangued us for an hour
a table at a time,
between screaming at the waitress
for poisoning her food.

Here two years
she told us of cities and countries she'd seen,
how her old neighbourhood had changed,
how her mother taught her Yiddish,
and her father's advice,
always to speak with appreciation
of places she'd just left.

When she'd emptied the café
despite hiding behind my papers
it was my turn.
But suddenly she was precise:

'I can tell you're busy,

just listen to this,

I won't take long.'

So I heard about the clever barman

on the second floor of a bus station in New York

who let her drink a beer on a hot day

between buses

though single women didn't drink in such places

in the early afternoon.

Saved her life!

'That's it!'

She stopped.

It took ten minutes of false starts

and pottering about

and gathering her possessions

and paying her bill

and muttered commentary

till she clumped out,

her life saved again

on another warm afternoon, between stops.

Jerusalem December 1990

Jerusalem farewell

On my way to Tel Aviv
facing backwards on the bus.
Peace be upon you, Jerusalem.
I am leaving,
descending,
backwards to Tel Aviv.

I remember you still
for the feelings you stirred within me
when I sang in your streets my songs of love,
innocent,
without price,
seeking in your air, Jerusalem …
seeking … your air.

Down, down I go
leaving you.
Soon your eyes will be hidden.

What is left beside the road
by one travelling backwards from Jerusalem?

Over there are memories,

there dreams,

resting,

crouched beneath their load,

waiting.

Will I return for them?

Past the Valley of Weeping

my eyes are already dry.

Arriving in Tel Aviv

backwards

empty.

Tel Aviv 5.12.90

Arabic class at Ulpan Akiva

For Shulamit Katznelson

> My morning stroll along the causeway
>
> that leads to the end of the world.
>
> In the distance, the seamless border.
>
> Sky touches sea
>
> air, water,
>
> water, air,
>
> hesitant
>
> guarded
>
> expectant.
>
> Yet water evaporates
>
> and air condenses,
>
> invisible exchanges
>
> and shared needs.
>
> Two kilometres
>
> through the sand-dunes of Netanya
>
> to the beginning of the world.

Netanya 28 November 1990

Language laboratory

You should not think we worship

if we sit enraptured

learn by heart each word

inflection

sing in praise

bewail the imperfection

in ourselves.

Our fathers also chanted

swayed in duty

sought to understand

to tease the very letters

into truth.

With less ambition now

we merely seek

to number

in another foreign tongue.

Butterflies

Leaves are tumbling into my breakfast coffee.

A hectoring voice lectures from the first-floor classroom.

And all around the butterflies on their maiden flight.

Already so much to complain about,

lecturer this, course that …

Such energy, life, spirit

and yet …

Other faces are etched beneath the smiles,

older souls tumbling back to earth,

self-conscious in jeans.

Such informality!

Redemption not yet come?

Perhaps this time.

Tel Aviv University 30 October 1990

Ants

The ants are building castles in my street.

Between the pavement tiles, little mounds of sand,

each neatly centre-pierced.

In stunted caverns they scurry to and fro

holding back the whispering ceaseless trickle

of their ever-crumbling walls.

Together, together,

faster now and faster!

Keep high the vault of heaven or we die.

The tiles already tilt beneath my feet.

Tread softly

lest we fall through heaven again

down,

down,

down

to the sand beneath.

Tel Aviv 30 October 1990

Dominant

The condoms

on the Netanya sand dunes

could prove to be an ecological hazard

to the ants.

Nevertheless

given the pace of change in ant technology

they may yet learn to accommodate

a large entrance hall

and rubber walls

in their condominiums.

Netanya 21.11.90

Yom Zeh L'Yisrael[1]

In any house
In Jerusalem
on Shabbat[2]
one may find a *minyan* [3]
praying
with *kavanah* [4]
according to the rules of *tefillah*.[5]

In any street
in Jerusalem
on Shabbat
one may find a *minyan*
playing with *kavanah*
according to the rules of Football.

It is not unusual
in either *minyan*
to play with one's head
or to pray with one's feet.

March 1972 Jerusalem

---

1. Literally, 'This day for Israel', the title of a poem/song celebrating the Shabbat, and sung after the evening meal on a Friday evening.
2. The 'Sabbath', from Friday evening to Saturday evening
3. A quorum of ten adult males, in traditional Jewish circles, required for a formal religious service
4. A word meaning either 'intention' or 'concentration', the necessary attitude when reciting the traditional prayers
5. 'Prayer', the formal traditional service.

Visitors

They sat on the beach

startlingly pale in the morning sun.

Side by side,

feet firmly planted

facing the sea

just out of reach of the lapping waves,

seemingly oblivious

to the movement around them.

If they spoke, none could hear.

Their silence was eerie

creating about them an aura

and a border

that all respected

and none wished to cross.

Did I say 'pale'?

Gleaming white is more correct.

And their stance?

A shocking unnatural symmetry.

As if they had stepped off another planet,

immaculately clad,

indifferent to the natural fauna

absorbed only in each other.

Alien

Superior.

Present.

How long they remained

I have no way of knowing.

Glancing back, I wished them well

and a successful conclusion

to their trip to the seaside,

two plastic garden chairs

in solemn communion

on Herzliya beach.

Netanya 27 November 1990

Visitors Revisited – Twenty-Seven Years Later

I saw them again today,
that same dazzling whiteness
artificial form
rigidity,
still masquerading
as innocent,
displaced,
garden chairs.

The water's edge must attract them,
but here is no Mediterranean Sea,
no endless vista.
Though skilfully composed,
contoured,
delicate,
a worthy imitation of some classical model,
when all is said and done,
this is, after all, merely a pond.

So why set down here?
Are they communicating with the carp?

Or simply admiring the dragonflies,
the strategically placed rocks,
exotic trees and bushes?
Unlike the visitors
though also foreign born,
these were all gifted,
formally and officially invited,
transplanted,
tended,
nurtured,
admired.

Admittedly,
today's intruders are not quite as before.
Do they evolve over time?
Metamorphose from plastic to metal mesh?
Or is this some kind of armour today?
What do they fear from us?

But once ignore these outer forms
the same unearthly stillness remains,
side by side,
silent,
purposeful,

staring,

jarring,

taunting us,

aggressively artificial

in this shrine to the organic,

to nature moulded by art.

Out of place before on a beach in Netanya,

again, they are utterly obtrusive

on this rare, sunny autumn day

in the farthest corner

of a vast public park,

at the Japanese garden

in unlikely Düsseldorf.

Is this their journey's end

or just another reconnaissance?

And when,

and where,

are they coming

for real?

Düsseldorf/Cordoba 21/10/2017

A genuine Japanese garden in Fukuoka.

Briefing

In welcoming you, my friends,
to our hospitality and culture
I must give you a warning.
Our customs and habits
though profoundly rooted
are hard to grasp.
Because few traditional taboos remain
anything may be taboo.
Where even our coffee is instant
you may be bewildered by the speed
of our welcome and our dismissal.

Do not let the casualness of our dress
or our overt sexuality
entice you.
The uncertainties they conceal
will betray you.

The terminology of greeting
'Good morning, how are you?'
is to be answered

'Fine, how are you?'
Both question and answer
are intended to reassure only
and should never be taken as an invitation
to elaborate.

Remember that silence here
conveys gravity,
politeness, culture.
Of the emotions
only boredom need be concealed.
However, no hint of cultural disdain
should be given.
Whatever shocks you
should be met with, at most,
a quizzical indifference.

Thus equipped
you will become guests
worthy indeed of us
your hosts.

Netanya, 22.11.90

Report to the committee

From personal observations in the class

while acknowledging the small size of the sample

and the lack of a control group

I would nevertheless postulate

that it is just as easy

and, indeed, just as difficult,

for Israeli Jews to learn Arabic

as it is for Arabs to learn Hebrew.

In the interests of maintaining a balanced view

I will repeat my conclusion

in the reverse order, namely

that it is just as difficult

and, indeed, just as easy

for Arabs to learn Hebrew

as it is for Israeli Jews to learn Arabic.

While it could be presumptuous

not to say unscientific

to extrapolate too much from these results

it might be legitimate to assume

that given similar social, educational
and cultural backgrounds
the two groups would display other common features
to a statistically significant degree.

In view of the unacceptability of these findings
to all parties
this report will remain classified
pending further....

Tel Aviv 19.11.90

Again Jerusalem, and again

Nevertheless

it is still possible to fall in love with

Jerusalem

all over again.

Despite everything.

Despite the fear in the streets of the old.

Despite the anger in the streets of the new.

For any hidden courtyard

any vista

any crowded corner

can snatch away your breath

by its sheer ...

density.

It is not the holiness,

too compromised,

nor its age alone.

It is something else:

a sad mocking at our pretensions

and a wonder at our dreams.

To have invested so much

in a couple of hills and valleys,

to have suffered so much to possess them
and done such harm to hold them
in the name of so many gods,
so much hope and greed.

So boast not of unity,
promise no eternity,
where Jerusalem is concerned,
for she will outlive our rhetoric
and lose even the memory of our passing –
another relic
for antiquarians to ponder
and archaeologists tenderly to reconstruct.

No,
better to tread softly,
woo her with tender care
and give the love we feel
to all her many children.

Portraits

He is still in the show-window off Jaffa Road.

That sixties face

marooned among the black hats of the eighties

encroaching fast.

Dark curly beard

hair already receding at twenty-five.

I'd forgotten the eyes were so intense.

What was he seeing so clearly

that young man

growing into Jerusalem

half-a-lifetime ago?

Today the greying hair and beard are cropped

executive style.

Glasses all the time

bifocals soon.

Are the eyes as intense?

Would he be picked again

from a thousand portraits

to sit in that window?

A different face

in a different Jerusalem.

Jonathan Magonet in 1967, photo taken in Jersusalem

Abroad

I have not yet mastered the beach

I have not yet mastered the beach.

This is no false modesty.

I seek no compliments.

I think I've got the hang of Factor Six.

I oiled myself frequently and thoroughly

sometimes with help for the awkward bits at the back.

And I did not burn.

True, I remained my usual pale self,

almost unchanged,

only my trunks outlined in red.

A victory, certainly,

in terms of hours, and indeed areas,

actually exposed.

But mastery?

No.

I've a tentative grasp of the relative expenditure of time

between beach, sea, shade, snack bar

(twice – a preliminary beer, a light lunch)

though perhaps I should swim longer distances

and with more zeal.

But all this is only dressing.

The ultimate ethic still eludes me.

How do they lie like that,

prone, unmoving, so vulnerable, for hours at a time?

Has it something to do with photosynthesis?

Solar energy?

Are they receiving subliminal messages from distant spheres?

Can they merely be getting a tan?

Is it, after all, just fun?

And why, why, won't they tell me?

Hell

Hell may be a place
where four narrow Mediterranean streets meet.
On each corner a bar where 'live groups' play nightly, loud,
classics of rock and roll.
People flow in and out of each bar in turn
in no recognizable sequence
pausing for variable intervals to drink
alone, or in pairs, or in groups,
at the tables that overflow each bar
into precise locations on the street.
Choice of seat determines which noise
predominates over the other three.
Conversation can only be carried on at a shout,
these punctuated bursts adding in no small measure
to the richness of the whole.

The passers-by are watched with interest
or curiosity, or indifference, or yearning, or lust,
by those seated,
who will in turn become the objects of such scrutiny.

Since individual words cannot be discerned
communication must be conveyed by signs, gestures,
the raising of an eyebrow, a smile or glassy stare.

The occasional fight,
the breaking of empty bottles or cracked glasses
into a box provided for the purpose,
or the random distribution of free passes
to a discotheque somewhere,
add momentary focuses of interest
to the otherwise conventional parade.

When drink or drugs prove too much for some
they may vomit in the corner
or sit on the curb, hunched up, oblivious, possibly weeping.
Acquaintances discuss them
with anxiety or anger down the street.

Apart from the occasional chanting
of a briefly-formed tribal group
belonging to one of the various nationalities or languages
that make up the populace,
little interrupts the timeless frenzy.
Newcomers are quickly assimilated,
former members soon forgotten.
The party is all.
Even those who merely observe the scene
find it difficult to depart.

Art disco

Does the presence

of attractive,

potentially-available women

enhance or limit

the possibilities of artistic expression

in a Disco?

(Or available men for women,

needless to say.)

Does the atavistic drive to hunt, mate,

bring to the dance an energy, urgency, an edge

it might otherwise lack?

Or is the search

for a hint of interest behind the cool mask

mere distraction,

even destructive to the creative purpose?

Is art, we ask,

merely display?

Alas,

other factors prove a greater hindrance.

The presence of other dancers is essential

for perspective,

but too many interfere with all but the most subtle

of movements.

And the music

oh! the music!

how seldom today

it

it

enlarges.

Ibiza 2.10.83

Resort blues

1. Morning Stroll

Harbor
Cafés
Check car number plates
Examine newspaper stand
Admire work of artists
Main square
Shopping streets
Compare prices of avocados
Inspect sea
from breakwater
from cove
Back by twelve
All in order
It is well to take one's responsibilities
seriously.

St. Tropez November 1969

2. Balance sheet

Item: two half-way decent poems
       and a few near misses.
Item: at least one hundred hours sleep.
Item: a down-payment on
       four sermons
       two articles and a lecture.
Item: five 'crimi's' read
       and a biography of a cancer victim,
       four clues completed
       in my ten-year-old Guardian crossword puzzle book
       (on the 'plane out).
Item: one successful game of Patience
       in only four attempts.
Item: one extended conversation in German
       two in French, one in English.
Item: one souvenir each for the kids.
Item: every side-street of Ibiza Town
       walked or glanced down.
       One old pair of sandals ruined.
Item: two apple pies, one chocolate cake
       and one plum cake in the Café Central.

Ibiza Town 1.9.96

Holding the Tiger

Her stage a board
no wider than the spread of her feet,
a candle before it,
a silvery-sided bowl.
In billowing black
three-pointed hat
black gloves
a glittering chain
dangling from one wrist
her face a painted clown
arms raised
motionless.

A clink of coins
her eyes blink open twice
warm smile
and slowly into motion,
elaborate bow
deeply to the right
slowly up
and slowly deep to the left
and back to rest.

Shyly the children
drop coins in her bowl
to give her life again.
Sometimes adults feed her hand
and elegantly
in mid motion
she lets the coins fall,
clink, to the bowl below.

Ibiza Town harbour,
Summer crowds
drawn
held
enchanted
released.
And she in turn is held
frozen in a camera flash
moving in a video's whirr
floating off a notebook page.

Ibiza Town 29.8.96

Another Moving Statue

Another moving statue
turned up today.
All in white
a Madonna of the islands
writhing slowly
to choral chants
pausing now and then
to blow bubbles
for children to catch.

He makes an impressive Madonna
though at six foot something
with craggy features
he lacks a certain charm.

I gather he tried to muscle in
on the black-garbed, slow-motion clown
over the way
pinching her pitch one evening.
She had the license so he had to move on.
Now he doesn't talk
when they pass in the street.

So the stage is set:

unforgiving Madonna

versus territorial clown,

whimsy at a hundred paces.

May the best mime win.

Ibiza Town 1.9.96

Resort Café

While the longhaired handsome one
chats up both women
in fractured Spanish
the quieter brunette eyes his lumpish companion
with unease.
Her vivacious friend keeps up the conversation
but she strays into boredom.
Without a common language
shy man retreats into familiar helplessness
looks away
lights his cigarette.

When the blonde goes to the ladies
longhair takes on the brunette
animates, entertains her,
his silent friend retreats further.

The blonde returns.
Shy man lights her cigarette,
shares a quick smile
but the moment is lost.

The men catch up a while, in German,

the women, in Italian.

Longhair goes to void his two beers.

Silence.

Time to look round the café

check watches

one a.m.

discuss which Disco to visit.

Returning he orders a fresh drink.

pointedly the blonde remarks on the time.

Longhair moves into overdrive

twice as amusing

eye-contact with both women

but the pauses between are longer.

He gambles on eating a hamburger …

The brunette orders fresh drinks.

A victory,

a sort of commitment.

but soon someone will have to move.

A sudden laugh

they exchange names

parody a hand-shake.

Longhair settles the bill

only two thousand so far.

They drift away towards

Es paradis terrenal.

Till two a.m.

it is half-price for couples.

Ibiza August 1988

Boredom

When all else fails

I can entertain myself

fishing bits of banana

out of the Sangria

with my straw.

I wouldn't put it on a level with

say

picking dead skin off my feet

but it has the advantage

of being publicly acceptable

and in some ways

quite a skill.

Reps

Across from my breakfast table

three bright blazers

pillar-box red, dazzling white and navy blue.

Three plump reps

in off-duty mode

comparing plane loads

salaries

and the hazards of the job.

Their plumage is too harsh

for Mediterranean pastels,

birds of paradise

marooned out of season

in a three-star gilded cage.

Polly's paying off her flat.

Molly's got a boyfriend down the coast.

Dolly's had enough and going home.

One fine day they will fly away

to Stansted, Gatwick or Luton

leaving behind the red, the white and the blue,

the cheery smiles and clipboards,

the radiant competence,

for Maisie, Daisy and Stacey.

The end of Empire

and the promise of village earth.

Palma Mallorca 5.1.97

Café Central

The Café Central
is about as *echt* as you can get
in a Mediterranean resort.
The toilet is spotless
and the hand-dryer works.
The heavy German ladies
who sit at kerbside tables
always take cream with their *Apfelkuchen*.

Its quiet tree-shaded courtyard
is an oasis
in a desert of Sangria-bars
and palaces of chicken and chips.
Here the clients are men
and whether Dutch, German or English
they share the same shaven heads
bushy moustache
Single ear-ring
tight shorts
and a great tan.

I never figured the reason they colonised the place.

Could be the decorum

of this shrine to *Gemütlichkeit*

or the charming *Kompetenz* of the waitress.

Only one woman,

a regular it seemed,

disturbed the restful hush

loudly addressing her young male friend.

(But perhaps being German

she simply felt at home.)

The place is so unlikely

so *Deutsch* and so gay

it stays in the mind,

a holiday puzzle

poignant, safe

and delightfully

zivilisiert.

Ibiza/London 25.9.96

Cappuccino

The waiters in Cappuccino,
smart in their black and white,
restlessly on the move,
are not like my granny.
For her an empty plate
should be filled;
for them, removed.

Does a shortage of crockery
inspire such zeal?
a policy of the house
to encourage a quicker turnover?
No matter.
Cappuccino
is a mood to savour,
a place to linger.
so in remembrance of pleasant hours
and out of respect for granny,
I shall nurse my coffee
till the end of this poem.

Palma, Mallorca 16 Jan 2002

Dubrovnik

Zudioska Street.
From an upper window:
'Synagoga?!!
Opposite Nada Café!!'

Remembered to kiss the *mezuzah*.
Above the upper staircase as you enter,
in Hebrew
'Blessed art thou as thou comest in.'

Behind a glass door on the landing
the Synagogue:
ark,
pictures
an old man dozes.
'Go away – closed!!'
'We want to see...'
'Cleaning!!'
'...the President.'
'Closed! Pesach!! Go away!!'

Above the door as you leave,
in Hebrew
'Blessed art thou as thou goest out.'
Forgot to kiss the *mezuzah*.

Happy hour

I'd missed the Tom Jones and Dolly Parton
lookalikes
though they did indeed lookalike
in last month's freebee resort magazine.
I successfully ran the gauntlet in the lobby,
avoiding:
day trips round the island,
see the coral reefs by submarine,
swim with the dolphins.
learn to scuba dive in three hours, only $75,
(paragliding looked tempting
till I thought about trying to land),
time-share apartments at special rates
plus, a one-time-only incentive offer
if you sign up at this very moment,
discount dinners with complementary cocktails
and a reduced entry to the show
of native dancers,
glass-eater and steel-drum player
at the Yellow Banana Nightclub.

I settled under the advertising umbrella

by the pool

(no diving, no watersports,

no open wounds allowed)

ignored the Bingo-caller

and piped zombie music,

sucked some ice and Rum

from my 'Miami Vice' cocktail,

second one free at 'Happy Hour',

and wrote a poem.

Princess Tower Hotel, Grand Bahamas 10.12.97

Bahama Mama

'I love you, Solly,

no, let me finish...

I love you, Solly,

but I keep doin' thin's to you

an' askin' forgiveness,

now is that love?'

A rush-mat screen

divided our part of the empty restaurant

from the bar

but the voices rang clearly through.

Four or five half-seen figures at the counter.

'The Bible says, if you believe...'

They argued the forgiveness of Jesus

and the riddle of Judas's death.

His betrayal was prophesied

so he had no choice.

Was he forgiven or not?

Solly banged on the counter for attention.

'What if you blasphemed the Holy Ghost?'

Only the sceptic

growling her four-letter word disagreements

broke the illusion

of a Sunday School exercise.

Just a typical December conversation

in downtown Grand Bahamas.

Bing's 'White Christmas' on the jukebox.

'Baywatch' on the silent TV screen.

Conch salad on the menu.

But behind the theology

'Who is a real Christian?'

'How come Paul was forgiven

when he killed so many Christians?'

did she maybe really love Solly

or was it just the Bahama Mama talking?

Grand Bahamas 8.12.97

Roma

    Foro di Augusto

    Foro di Cesare

    Foro di Nerva

    Foro Romano

    Foro Traiano

Across the road from the remains

of the Flavian Amphitheatre

('popularly known as the Colosseum')

where Christians were thrown to the lions

('though the scholars generally doubt

that it was here that the Christians were killed')

a cheery little old woman

admired by Japanese tourists,

tosses scraps of bread

to the pussy-cats of Rome.

    Basilica di Massenzio

    Basilica di San Giovanni

    Basilica di San Lorenzo

    Basilica di San Paolo

    Basilica di San Pietro

Saint Peter's Square

holds more than the Colosseum

('Even 50,000 people

could "enjoy" the fights of the gladiators.'

'The Pope can have an audience of 150,000.')

On the other hand, it does lack facilities

for staging naval battles.

140 saints atop Bernini's 'majestic colonnade'

('completed in 1657 at the height of the
counter-reformation.')

stand with arms poised

thumbs presumably at the ready.

   Galleria Borghese

   Galleria Colonno

   Galleria Communale

   Galleria Doria Pamphili

   Galleria D'Arte Antica

   Galleria Nazionale

If one is running the world

it must be nice to bring a few souvenirs back,

and the odd bit of local art

helps impress visitors.

I suppose it's all a matter of taste

nowadays.

Musei Capitolini

Musei Vaticano

Museo Barracco

Museo Nazionale delle Arti

Museo Nazionale d'Arte Orientale

Museo Nazionale di Villa Giulia

Muzeo Nazionale Romano della Terme

Et Cetera.

    Rome Feb 1978

(European Judaism Vol 12, No 1, Spring 1978 p33)

Novotel

    I leave behind a presence

    unmade bed

    damp towels

    half a tube of shampoo

    a coffee stain

    a dab of toothpaste in the sink

    the print of a finger.

    Someone was here

    and is gone.

    I leave behind an absence

    dreams unremembered

    warmth from a body

    moisture in the air

    images blanked from the screen

    the echo of a wake-up call

    the snick of a closing door.

    Someone was here

    but is gone.

Amsterdam 5.4.06

Artefacts
For Ken Adam

    Outside the city wall
    on a ledge overlooking the gorge
    someone has planted a garden
    of gutted washing machines and cookers
    of rusted oil drums
    now filled with earth,
    now brimming with the green of leaves.

    Across the gorge
    upon the face of the old city
    a film company erects
    the walls
    and towers
    and gates
    of Jerusalem
    in fibreglass
    moulded, coloured and aged
    to blend, seamless,
    onto the crumbling façade.

    Yet which is the greater art
    bringing life to the dead
    or bringing the dead to life?

Matera 24 April 1984

*Technical adviser and briefly performer
(I married King David, Richard Gere, to Michal, Cherie Lunghi)
for the film 'King David'.[1]*

---

1. For an entertaining account of advising on the movie, see Chapter 6, 'My part in the fall of 'King David' - the Bible goes to the Movies' in my A Rabbi Reads the Bible (SCM Press, London, 1991/2004).

Moments

We do a great goodbye

time

distance

absence

dissolving the constraints

that other loyalties impose.

Hello is good as well

a rush of joy

a sweetness

overcoming

time

distance

absence,

making airports,

railway stations,

doorsteps

intimate

intense.

When together

we practice

caution

careful not to come too close

assume too much

intrude too far,

almost lovers become friends.

When apart

a little fantasy

some longing

cross the space

from phone to phone,

the heart grown fonder

friends become almost lovers.

But oh how sweet the hello,

how warm the goodbye.

Street Scene

The car pulled into the parking bay.

She got out, angry, in tears,

plump in tee-shirt and jeans,

and strode off down the street.

He shouted her name,

stood by the open door,

slim, smart in a black suit.

She kept on walking,

crossing the road.

He waited

then closed the door

beeped it locked

and followed,

catching up on the corner

a block away.

He spoke, his hands by his sides,

hers waved in reply, emphatic.

My lift arrived and we drove away.

What had he said or done?

What were they to each other?

Did they reconcile?

Five-thirty-five on a warm spring Monday

on Goetheallee in Göttingen,

a Prévert poem come to life,

the sentiment lost in translation.

Göttingen 10.5.04

New York Interlude

1.
It's forty years too late
to be sitting here
in the Village
somewhere off
McDougal Street and Bleecker
imagining how it was
how it must have been
back then.

Sixties nostalgia on the speaker.
Forty blends of tea to choose.
Lap tops open
on every table,
cell phones chirping,
as if
here
is only a portal
to somewhere else.

My own sixties songs
were born in Jerusalem,
London, Bendorf
adolescent wisdom
set to New York rhythms.
Too comfortable then
to run away from home,
too timid
to risk other worlds,
not driven by the passion to create,
not even a troubadour's bravado.

Not so very different today
in this tea room
off McDougal Street and Bleecker
forty years on,
still just passing through
but at least
for this brief moment
here.

2.

I think I'm developing blisters.

New York avenues are long

and places to sit few.

When you're over sixty

journeys are measured

to the next Starbucks

and the rest-room queue.

New York/Strasbourg/London 3.10.08

Cities
© *Words and Music Jonathan Magonet*

    London town where I was born
    Streets are damp, and people yawn
    Lonely children, plastic scorn
        But if my head should rule my heart
        Of London I could be a part.

    Paris elegance is cold
    Children in the streets are old
    Weary games of words are sold
        But if my head should rule my heart
        Of Paris I could be a part.

Berlin in a brittle haze
Remembers vanished golden days
Ghostly martial music plays
>But if my head should rule my heart
>Of Berlin I could be a part.

Amsterdam has beauty rare
Streets of water, singing air
People once knew how to share
>But if my head should rule my heart
>Of Amsterdam could be a part

New York's chimney homes are stark
Grubby streets where people bark
Anger lurking in the dark
>But if my head should rule my heart
>Of New York I could be a part.

Jerusalem is growing young
Richest songs are still unsung
Harmonised in every tongue
>And if my heart should rule my head
>Jerusalem is where I'm led.

Jerusalem 1967

Portraits

Inflight

To you, madam,

my neighbour on Pan Am flight 101

Heathrow to JFK

one Monday in March

Cabin class

I dedicate this poem.

And to your husband,

German?

A doctor – he will lecture soon in Heidelberg

who listened with such patience

to your opening forty-minute tirade.

Yes, you were definitely booked in seat 6F

an aisle seat,

clipper class,

arranged before you left New York.

Yes, you did want to sit next to him

but could he not understand that you meant

on each side of the aisle

not scrunched up in a middle seat

especially among these yokels from the country

on some cheap package flight

when you had paid full fare!

And you had hoped to rest on this flight

to arrive in New York refreshed

for two seats at the opera tonight

Don Carlos

and you'd missed it twice before.

The first forty minutes of seven hours.

Between the pauses

when he slept or you slept

(you'd seen the movie on the flight out)

we heard the saga of his relations in Vienna,

the girl who nearly married the brother

of an Indian airline pilot who only wanted

a mother for his two children.

And how could he be planning a new trip

to Europe

at that very moment before they'd even landed

instead of waiting till you got home

without asking you about it first

without leaving you space for yourself

to sort out your medical problems

a thyroid test

(the doctor had insisted)

and some more intimate, internal trouble

you did not wish to discuss

at this moment in time,

and your dancing lessons,

newly begun,

and your decision generally to relax more,

to enjoy New York,

to 'initiate a change' in your life.

In between the strident whine

cuddling him and cooing

and crossing and uncrossing

and lifting onto the seat ahead

and re-crossing again

your extraordinary, demented,

restless lets,

skirt hiked up to the thighs.

(Clearly not Jewish but Protestant

said a sympathetic New York friend later

– the exposure of the legs, he explained).

Such energy, such need,

such magnificently, unremitting,

blatant, self-centredness.

Wise to have picked a European husband.

You gobbled your in-flight food

(forgive my noticing

but everything was somehow on display)

evidence of an older, deeper hunger?

If you read this

take my advice

and double check the thyroid

but meanwhile

have a nice day!

New York April 1986

Broadway and 65th

The guy who runs Lincoln Center

from his ice-cream parlour across the road

has a banana-split belly

and knows how to spot a panhandler.

'You just have to look at their shoes.

I've seen one guy in a tuxedo and bare feet!'

As a philosopher, he is against Pride.

'Look at the French.

They hate us Americans.

They can never forgive what Truman did for De Gaulle.

They treat us like dirt.

If I had my way I'd put such a tariff on their goods

they'd never get into the country!'

Between placing customers

and figuring which show people will be in today

he monologues with his waitresses,

smart in white blouses, black slacks,

on techniques of the trade

on their private pains and diseases

on the name of that actress

well-stacked

used to be in all those Sinatra-Dean Martin movies

what was her name?

A lot of managers come in.

Sure, I get offered complementary tickets.

One guy told me: Ask at the box office.

Four tickets in the name of 'Irv'.

I was embarrassed to ask.

Is that I-R-V or E-R-V?

Sure, they were there.

Twenty dollars apiece.

Some complementary!

What's that?

He wants half a tea-bag?

That's OK.

He's the customer!

New York April 1986

Helena

    In winter she makes the bags

    and necklaces, earrings,

    displayed on a stall in the square.

    Rumour has it she's a belly-dancer too

    in a club in Portamao.

    And somewhere in Lisbon

    there's a nine-year-old boy

    living with her father

    and the 'young wife'.

    A long way from Morocco,

    ten years here,

    a broken marriage behind her.

    (Portuguese, born in Angola,

    never got used to Europe,

    drugs ...)

    Once she spent a month in an Ashram

    meditated

    felt herself leaving her body.

    'they gave me a mantra

    and it became a line in space.'

The hour her grandmother died
she saw her in a dream,
her face younger but somehow the same.
One day she'll go to India
and learn their religion.

Now she's here.
She shrugs,
cuddles her girlfriend
or the tall Swiss boy
who doesn't like to make plans
or the Rhodesian she lives with
(wants to start a crayfish farm).
In the Disco later
on the floor
in her dark Sephardi eyes was pain
older than her own.

She is grey
For Sarah Kamin *z'l*

    She is grey

    grey

    death is leeching the colour

    from her face.

    Note the swollen ankles

    the concealing head-scarf

    the matchstick frame

    so frail.

    She is still there within

    warm

    precise

    tender.

    The sketches are too pretty.

    That is not her beauty.

    Capture instead the friends around her

    whose turn it is to give

    and share

    and hold

    and wait it out.

Capture the calm

the laughter

the softness of memories

the ebb and flow of pain

the life still about her

and within her.

Not that grey, grey face,

not yet,

not ever.

Jerusalem 13.8.89

Arc poetry reading
For Riva Rubin

Fourteen, or was it sixteen, poets

reading

-in the café beforehand

we weren't sure who was turning up.

Fourteen, or was it sixteen, poets.

No white page,

conventional print,

to hide behind.

Body,

face,

dress,

voice,

exposed.

Poems become again persons.

Fourteen, or was it sixteen, poets.

Secrets, pain,

observed,

recorded,

honed,

nuanced,

concealed.

Fourteen, or was it sixteen, poets,

recited,

read,

declaimed,

performed,

risked

and gave

into our clutching hands,

devouring hearts.

Fourteen, or was it sixteen, poets,

or was it only

one?

Tel Aviv 12.12.90

Bal Paré

A quiet night at the Ball Paré.
The DJ seems his usual cheery self
perched in his organ loft above the bar.
The usual medley of five -
umpapa umpapa
slow, becoming fast
with the odd waltz in between.
'Tanz mit mir Corinna.'
'You're my heart, you're my soul.'
'Einfach da zu sein.'
'Sempré, sempré tu.'
Sometimes quite suggestive
in a jolly sort of way:
'Erst ein Cappuccino
dann ein bisschen Vino
und dann du!'

It's a nicer place than some.
Fewer expectations,
not the urgency of the disco set.
A different sort of display:
the art of the quick-step
breathtaking turns

hip-hip-hopping on tippy-tip-toe,
bodies a little past their prime
but what style!

For the 'green widows'
a night away from the telly
at a place where a woman may come alone.
A chat with the girls
joke about the men
enjoy a dance
who knows....
For the ageing 'swingers',
a break from the bed-sit
little risk of refusal for at least one medley
a few moments of closeness
and, after all, who knows....

At the turn of the hour the women may invite
but seldom do.
Older traditions prevail
proprieties are still observed
even on a quiet night
at the Bal Paré.

Bremen 7.8.92

Waiting for Rosi
For Rosi Dasch

Waiting for Rosi

is no problem

for we know she will arrive

come hell or high water

whirling in

from somewhere else

she also had to be.

Rosi creates time for others:

time to imagine

the hopeless pupil,

the business calls

she had to make,

the inevitable friend,

she met in the street,

the rehearsal that ran late

because

it started late...

How many lifetimes

can Rosi pack into one?

But how many Rosis

could we meet in a lifetime?

So gratefully we wait

for the tremor in the air

that announces her coming

and taking a deep breath

we leap aboard

to find the little bit of space

still free.

Wuppertal 15.6.96

Hanging out with Hesh
For Hesh Grinspoon

>Hanging out with Hesh
>is fun.
>All you need is
>a flexible wardrobe
>and a great memory
>for what got left behind
>in what car
>what house
>what country.
>Did I mention
>the stamina of an athlete
>a line in snappy repartee
>and a modest degree of masochism?
>
>It is advisable to be
>nutritionally correct
>but occasionally self-indulgent.
>Eat as he says
>if not always as he does.
>For Hesh is hungry
>for a different kind of food.
>People and ideas nourish him
>as he in turn nourishes others.

Returning to the subject of clothes
do not let the floppy hat
the awesome shirts
the hiking hardware
fool you.
They are part of his disguise
as an urban innocent,
just a folksy old boy
- with a steel-trap mind.
Part patron, part artist,
he is still surprised
at what he too can create.

Given his advancing years
and enviable energy
he is aging disgracefully well.
So it is just conceivable
though the thought itself would embarrass him
that he is well on his way
from street-smart to sage
from shrewd to wise
one springy stride at a time.

Crestview Circle, Longmeadow, MA 24.8.98

Shabbat Conversations at Sami's
For Sami Barth's 40th

'Let our teacher explain to us...'
    'We can deduce...'
'You may be misled to think this but...'
    'Then how much more so in the case that...'
'Whence do we know...?'
    'Is it not self-evident?'
'But does it not also say...?
'   'That is why the text explicitly states...'
'I might suppose, but...'
    'Do not read this but that...!'
'But surely we have learnt in a Baraita...!'
    'There is no contradiction:
    one is before this, the other is after this...'
'Just the opposite seems to be the case!'
    'Just as here it means this, so there it means this.'
'Is it possible that....?'
    'What it really means is...'
'I need this proof but it is lacking...'
    'The matter is like the following story...'
'Dare we suggest that....?'
    'No, it is necessary in the following case....'
'Does the master not hold...?'
    'It appears to be reasonable that....'
'Let it stand...'

Musicians

Tubby Hayes/Klook's Kleek 19.6.64

The band

It was Christmas Eve in Toby's
on the southern Algarve coast
and the wind was chill on the quayside
and we'd drunk our final toast.
But though the place was empty
it wasn't time to quit
for a bunch of old musicians
were finishing their set.

I don't recall their names now
or what they called the band
some silly-sounding title
only they could understand.
They must have got together
to have a little fun
or show they still could cut it
and stand there in the sun.

And sure, their jokes were lousy
and they hit some notes too soon
and the mikes were playing havoc
and they sometimes lost the tune

but they didn't let it phase them
and they gave it all they had
and the energy was flowing
and you came out feeling glad.

And once or twice they gripped you
when the guy on tenor blew
or they played an old French love song
and talked the lyric through.
So those who walked out early
or weren't too much impressed
they had a pleasant evening
but maybe missed the best.

So, it wasn't merely charity
or simply feeling kind
but the way they loved their music
that kept them on your mind.
The streets were almost empty
on the way to my hotel,
from the church came voices singing
a final, sweet Noel

Albufeira 27.12.86

To Jonathan,
Can you do this in oil?
Al Cohn

Al Cohn/Half-Note Club, New York 16.7.65

Sonny Stitt/Ronnie Scott's Club 4.5.64

The duo quiche

The Duo Quiche
are performing tonight
in the hotel bar.

He is on keyboards
expressionless.
The relentless rhythm
the melody line and bass
are all pre-programmed,
so his must be the out-of-tempo
off-key runs
electronically transmuted
into trumpet, piano or sax.

She looks to be in her forties
dressed today in her simple spangled black.
The photos on the poster
had promised her in several
cabaret performances:
Evita, Piaf, 'folklore'
and something a little naughty

in black stockings and suspenders.
But facing her elderly, unresponsive
multination audience
she looks understandably bored
and performs like a perfect extension
of the keyboard.

After five numbers
including Guantanamera
pounded remorselessly into oblivion
they stop
and the silence is nectar
their one welcome moment of art.

    Remember Guantanamera?
    Pete Seeger live somewhere
    and the hope that a song
    could change the world?
    Remember?
    Was its fate already sealed
    at that moment, Pete?

And what of the hopes of the Duo Quiche?

What dreams of stardom

got damaged along the way

in one-night stands

in sleepy bars

in three-star hotels

in out-of-season resorts?

And yet of all the songs

in all the world

on which to take revenge

for all that never happened,

why Guantanamera?

Palma, Mallorca 6.1.97

Mark Murphy/Ronnie Scott's Club 27.9.64

Stan Tracey/Ronnie Scott's Club 3.7.64

Hedy's Song
For Hedy West
© Words and music Jonathan Magonet

Sing your song, soft above the city noise

And let me ride, warm within your voice

Tales of peacocks and pins

And love that wins.

Weave your spell, conjure up another day

Hard time blues, little work and little pay

Ghosts of mighty men

Live again.

Catch the echo of a poet's call

Wistful pictures shyly float and fall

Then the laughter rings

Banjo sings.

London 1968

The Best

Neville, Neville,

I envy you the night you stood in

for George Shearing

for two sets at a jam session

in London in the fifties

even though you were only

a semi-pro.

'Playing with the best

brings out the best in you!'

The British colony's own

resident

pensioned

semi-pro

mainstream

jazz band.

'Charity performances

every Monday night'.

You're looking forward to July
when George Chisholm comes
for two weeks.
'He must think we're good
to want to play with us again.'

Thanks for letting me sit in
on harmonica
for two numbers, Neville.
I hope I'll remember it
thirty years from now
that night at the Casino Bar, San Clemente
in the eighties.
Playing with the best
brings out the best in you.

Minorca 26.3.1980

Zoot Sims/ Half-Note Club, New York 16.7.65

Dick Morrissey/Ronnie Scott's Club 20.10.65

Talking to the boys of the band
For Pearl Bailey
©Words and Music Jonathan Magonet

I may be singin' or I may be chattin'

I'm in L.A or even old Manhattan

Doing TV or on another one night stand

Chorus:

Don't get me wrong, but while I'm singing you my song

I'm really talking to the boys of the band.

It's in the timing and it's in the pacing

Sleepwalking or downhill-racing

With just a drummer or a fellow with a baby grand.

May not be moving but I'm always dancing

It only works when you're in there chancing

Letting it take you to where you never planned.

To sing a love-song anyone will do

But to make the words come out true

Takes an old broad to really understand.

The band are playing for one another

You're just a stranger if you ain't their brother

'Cos nothing else matters when you're up here on the stand.

London 31.5.80

Jimmy Deucher/Ronnie Scott's Club 3.7.64

Jimmy Witherspoon/Ronnie Scott's Club 9.8.64

Bibo's Song

© *Words and Music Jonathan Magonet*

Verse 1 and Chorus

Bibo is my name and I'm a band

Got a thousand tunes in my hand

And I've played the coast of Spain I've been around

And my agent's got me booked for a winter in Berlin or is it Rome....?

2. All I need's a piano and a chair.

Doesn't matter much if no-one's there

'Cos I've got a big selection I can play

Fit for any clientele or any time of night or day...

3. Find me in a hotel in the spring,

just before the season gets in swing.

Pretty soon and I'll be moving on

There's a beat group coming in and summer people like a different song...

4. If there's something you would like to hear,

Say the name or hum it to me clear.

I'll try to play it nice and play it true,

And if you come again I'll recall your face and play it just for you...

Hotel Mediteran, Budva 11.4.76

Roland Kirk/Ronnie Scott's Club 29.10.64

GHOSTWALK AND OTHER POEMS   JONATHAN MAGONET

Ronnie Scott/Ronnie Scott's Club 3.7.64

Allen Ganley/Ronnie Scott's Club 17.11.64

Guitar Player
© Words and Music Jonathan Magonet

I'm playing my guitar and it's a quarter to three
Waiting for the clients to go home.
There's a lady in the corner with an eye on me
And it's time to say hello or maybe roam.
'Cos I'm an independent fellow
And I've seen it all before
And no lady is a lady in this place
But the night is not yet over
And the music's flowing fine
And losing out again is no disgrace.

It's a seedy sort of setup on the wrong side of town
And the manager's a loser all the way
And though I wouldn't like to put the customers down
They don't really understand the things I play.
But now I'm not so fussy and the hours suit me fine
And I sort of like the stories that I hear.
If you want someone to listen while you tell the way it was
I only cost the price of a beer.

I'm not very sure if this is really my place
Or maybe I have missed the proper boat

An awful lot of water passed over my head
And I was happy just to learn to float.
I've seen the guys who only tried to get far ahead
And I've seen the ones who tried to settle down
And though it's kind of quiet when I'm back in my room
There are places that they know me round town.

This wasn't meant to be the tale of my life
And maybe it won't get me very far
But everybody tells me all the troubles they've seen
And sometimes I just talk to my guitar.
So if you're ever passing and you feel like a drink
And you're not too shy to stand me a round
I'll play you something pretty, we'll talk for a while
And maybe we can make a good sound.

I'm playing my guitar and it's a quarter to three ......

Jerusalem/Arnhem 20/8/71

Donald Byrd/Ronnie Scott's Club 3.7.64

GHOSTWALK AND OTHER POEMS   **JONATHAN MAGONET**

J.J.Johnson/Ronnie Scott's Club 6.9.64

Leo Wright, Bundesallee, Berlin 27.8.64

Freddy Hubbard/Ronnie Scott's Club 17.11.64

Japan

A car horn honked!

A car horn
honked!
Can you imagine such a thing?
The shock of it!
Three months of overwhelming politeness.
Silent cars,
virtual pedestrians
on these narrow lanes,
putting to shame
the pushiness of cyclists
weaving their aggressive way
where we cautiously walk.

A-san took a left
onto the main road,
slipping in front of oncoming B-san,
sliding to the farther lane.
A poor move
dangerous

badly timed
inelegant
distinctly
un-Japanese.
No wonder B-san,
surprised
shocked
distressed
actually
honked!

Back home
B would have chased A
at least to the next lights
honking
blaring
cursing
raging.
But here
a honk, yes,
but hardly more than a beep.

Outrage
without rage,
or so it seems.
And yet
what self-discipline,
what banked passions,

concealed,

suppressed,

lie behind that single sound.

Over in a second,

reverberating for eternity.

Fukuoka 30.4.10

Fireflies

How sad that

'the random motion of particles'

(what was it called?)

was all that came to mind

in the darkness.

No childhood memory

as fireflies

flared

darted

danced

darkened

and flared again

in their tiny valley

of streams

and waterfalls.

Not the magic of nature

but the logic

of elementary physics

('Brownian motion'

or 'pedesis')

my legacy

of an urban childhood.

How sad to mistake

the croak of frogs

for crickets,

unable to distinguish

what my companions notice today

as the first scent of summer.

I envy a childhood

which knows the names of special days,

excursions for

'hanami',

to sit beneath cherry blossoms,

for 'hotaru-gari'

watching fireflies

in their brief, bright interval of life.

I shall miss

'momijigari'

this year,

when autumn colours change,

but today I noticed

how red are the flowers

in the bushes on the path

to my scholarly office.

And I look each day from the bridge

for my white wading bird

when the tide recedes.

Perhaps there's hope for me,

twice a foreigner

in this land.

Fukuoka 11.6.2010

Hanami – cherry blossom viewing party
Hotaru gari – catching fireflies
Momijigari – viewing autumn foliage

Rain

I awake to the urgent summons of the rain;

heavy splashes on my balcony,

and beyond

a lighter whispered sighing

now rising in volume and tempo

humming

drumming

crashing

waterfalls of sound,

then,

just as suddenly,

diminishing,

while single drips

and the wash of tyres on the road

add new rhythms and tones;

a symphony for wind and percussion,

the morning rehearsal

for another rainy-season day

in Fukuoka.

Fukuoka 29.6.10

Cicada

In this country

which still has seasons

the song of the cicada

 is heard in the land.

The rainy-season is past

and the summer has come

with its stupefying heat.

No beloved,

actual or metaphorical,

comes skipping over Kyushu's hills.

Israel's God

will have to find a niche here

like all the many others.

Being 'jealous' or 'zealous'

cuts little ice

where temples and shrines abound

for any and every need,

spiritual or material.

The Psalmist prayed
from a dry and weary land
where there is no water,
but rain here hardly warrants a prayer
unless it be for it to stop.
The rice growers
have a formidable lobby
in the heavenly court
so, a seasonal discomfort
is best disregarded
for the sake of the collective good.

The drumming of the rain
now the harsh trilling of cicadas,
Japan has a music
all its own.
Back home
the traffic on Finchley Road
will have to suffice
till next year.

Fukuoka 20.7.2010

A night time stroll

I happened to walk through Nakasu
the other evening,
a very peaceful stroll.
Actually, the street was rather busy,
lots of traffic and noise and neon lights,
with pretty girls handing out cards
to passers-by,
for a party or a meal,
or whatever it was they were offering.
But they never approached me
so, it was a very peaceful stroll.

Of course, I did wonder why
they never approached me.
Perhaps they looked at my grey hair and beard,
my serious demeanour,
and thought:
the old boy's not really the type
for a party or a meal
or whatever it was they were offering.
He might drop dead with a heart attack
and then where would we be!
Better leave him alone.
So, it was a very peaceful stroll.

It's a pity really.

After all, I still enjoy a party
if it's not too rowdy,
and a meal,
if it's not too heavy,
and perhaps
whatever else it was they were offering.
But now I'll never know
and that too is a bit of a pity.
After all,
half the fun of travelling is meeting new people,
experiencing the unknown,
but first they have to want to let you in.

(Netsuke Nation)
Fukuoka

The Chapel of St. Nico

The Chapel of St. Nico
is dedicated to no god,
makes no theological claims,
seeks only to fulfil the expectations
of its shareholders,
and the immediate needs
of clients who use its,
admittedly excellent,
facilities and services.

A stunning organ,
stained glass windows
that adjust to
daylight
twilight
midnight
at the press of a button
or high-tech equivalent.

The sound system can accommodate
the most sacred
or most secular
occasions

with equal effectiveness.
No vulgar buzzing announces
the start of the programme.
rather a carillon of bells
to rival Notre Dame
calls us to attention,
reminds us to prevent the intrusion
of lesser music from cell phones,
and sets the ecclesiastical tone.

What if the gothic columns
are plastic,
and the rented wedding minister
is mildly embarrassed by his role,
the couple get their money's worth
of ambience and ceremony
appropriate to the occasion,
and a splendid meal downstairs.

Regrettably its location
on the third floor of a high-rise
in downtown Hakata
prevents the release
of balloons or doves
at the climactic moment.

For this feature
clients are better served
by the wedding company
using the picturesque
mock Mediterranean cathedral
in Nishijin,
past the Fukuoka tower,
beside the artificial beach.

The cross and candlesticks
are tastefully arranged
around the altar with its open book,
possibly even a Bible.
Unfortunately,
not knowing its function,
the impressive stand and box
at the entrance,
marked 'Prière',
has no slot for charitable donations.
Perhaps they are included
in the overall price.

Fukuoka, Japan 22.4.2010

Everything changes in Fukuoka

Everything changes in Fukuoka,
in the blink of an eye
for the visitor,
though it's nine months
for the locals.

The one hundred yen shops,
actually one hundred and five
at the till,
now one hundred and eight
with the new tax,
have become a chain
the 'life co-ordinate shop'.

So, gone the random
unexpected discoveries,
squeezed into a corner,
hardware or stationery,
floppy hats or garden gnomes,
now sorted and sanitised
in the perfection of the new,

spacious,

fully comprehensive

pastel emporium

(though the plastic floor mop

snaps too easily at the joints

and the socks grow holes

too quickly.)

But why mock

such brilliantly executed

(made in China)

calculated practicality,

such quality,

value for money,

such retailing brilliance?

Sometimes I miss

the local supermarket

around the corner

the new store replaces.

For some reason

toilet rolls

tissues and paper kitchen towels

cannot yet be packaged

for one hundred and eight yen.

A shop, of course, is one thing.

If only it was possible

with such flair,

such conviction,

so comprehensively,

and so cheaply,

to co-ordinate a life,

even allowing for tax.

Fukuoka July 1 2014

In the Suburb of Machida

In the suburb of Machida

at a crossroad

stands each and every day

an attractive young woman

in the black jacket and skirt

high heels

of an office lady,

perhaps with an umbrella

against the summer sun

or winter rain.

Periodically relieved by a colleague

identically clad

she supports a placard

its message in bright colours

plain, for all to see.

As long as life goes on

in its untroubled way,

the odd earth tremor notwithstanding,

in this lively bustling suburb

of Tokyo,

twenty yards away

there will stand

the people's palace

proclaiming the promise and hope

of pachinko.

Let all who fear

the end of days

take heart,

for while she,

or one of her colleagues,

stands steadfast at her post

in the suburb of Machida

pachinko will remain confined

within those palace walls.

The slots will sing their siren song

and all will be well.

But should the day ever come,

which the gods of chance forbid!!

when that iconic figure departs

from her allotted place

at the crossroad

in the suburb of Machida

then tremble,

for pachinko has broken free,

is now at large throughout the world.

And, as every gambler,

not in denial,

knows

it is never the players

but always the House

that wins.

Tokyo 2.6.2015

GHOSTWALK AND OTHER POEMS   JONATHAN MAGONET

ジョナサン・マゴネット
小林洋一 [編]

ラビの聖書解釈
ユダヤ教とキリスト教の対話

新教出版社

ジョナサン・マゴネット (Jonathan Magonet)
1942年ロンドンに生まれる。ロンドン大学医学部を卒業後、ラビへの転身を志してロンドンのレオ・ベック大学で学び、71年にラビに任職。74年にドイツのハイデルベルク大学で旧約聖書学により博士号を取得。レオ・ベック大学教授として聖書学を講じ、また同学長を歴任した。宗教間対話に精力的に取り組む。

Rabbino Seishokaishak:
Yudaiyakuo to
Kiristokuo no Taiwa
Jonathan's collected Japanese
lectures on Bible and
Interfaith Dialogue.
One day he hopes to be able
to read them.

Haiku 26.3.10

1.

やまの　きり

とおくに　のぼる

まちの　いし。

Mountain mist
far away emerge
a city's stones.

2.

びじゅつかん

はるの　はな　しぬ、

きゃくは　みる。

Art museum
spring flower dies
visitors observe.

3.
きょうの　あめ
おてらの　ねこは
うたいます。

Today's rain,
the temple cat,
sings.

Reflections

Jewish Writers in Concert

    evening of ugly equations

    reluctant heirs
    almost wrestle our shadow
    but slide away
    feigning the family limp.

    evening of ugly equations

    dead-alive
    nightmare-dream
    blackness-sun
    grave-garden

    scratch our sores
    cry loneliness

soldier songs

wild applause

in vain our bribe of poems

stumbles ahead

the simple too easy

truth burns.

air smells

hunter's hate recalled

nestles warm

like a second skin

on orphan hands.

run away

but louder pulses nagging life

whole charade to teach us …

death?

exile still a state of soul.

24.1.68

Waiting

Waiting for someone
who does not appear
is a quite special skill.

Of course it depends
how much is invested
in the meeting
but the salient points
remain the same.

How late is late?
When does doubt
become unease
become certainty?
How many others
have similar vigils
nearby?

How soon
does the casual awareness
of another's tardy partner
elicit hopes or fantasies
to be dashed
when he appears?

Double-dashed.

Those who wait
know
in their heart of hearts
it was a mistake
mischance
easily remedied.

So the smile
though strained
remains.
Some gestures
tell indifferent passers-by
that nothing is amiss.

A last casual glance
at the watch,
tap it, perhaps.

Offer the nearest
now familiar face
a reassuring glance
and limp
into the setting sun.

Ibiza September 1983

Little people

Those little people are everywhere now.
It's too late!
With their terrible certainty
and mute dominion,
their either/or
black/white
do/don't
no middle ground for them.

Their shapes may change,
a detail here and there,
but it's still those matchstick legs
that moon for a face
a skirt suggesting gender
arms in dumb extension.

Nowhere is free of them.
They hang around toilets
with their blatant sexism
men only!
women only!

Who do they think they are?

On every street
whole families on parade
demanding we make way
for their school children
their old ones with sticks.
They congregate on corners
in technicolour!
Green for 'go'.
Red for 'stop'.
Have they no shame?

They'll be in our homes next!
speechless,
nagging,
watching.

I tell you,
you'll notice them now!

Tel Aviv 11.11.90

For the sake of the poem

> For the sake of the poem
> it would be better
> if you did not reply
> leaving me free to speculate
> to my heart's discontent
> about your silence.
> Then scenarios galore
> from dramatic to absurd
> could fill the space
> where your presence
> your absence
> hovers.
>
> For the sake of the poem
> memories must suffice
> of an empathy,
> was it only imagined?
> an attraction
> undoubted
> another mind

challenging,

and endless possibilities

tinged, as always,

with an essential irony.

For the sake of the poem

how marvellous the chance

to indulge

in feelings unexpressed,

to lament

an intimacy unrealised,

to taste a regret

hovering on anger,

a smidgen of guilt,

a trace of self-pity,

and, when the humour has departed,

a wisp of sorrow

with nowhere to go.

For the sake of the poem....

For the sake of the poet

a reply would be welcome!

Once across the sea

Once across the Sea
there is no more return.
No dried-out seabed path
leads back to Egypt.
And on the shore too many dead
defend the way.

Even looking back is a risk.
So many ancient shores
bear monuments of salt,
memorials to olden times,
old pains reduced to ritual and rote.
Why cross the Sea
just to linger on the shore?

Yet still the water calls,
now shimmering and sparkling in the sun.
Who needs another wilderness to cross?
Better rest awhile
breathe deeply
calm that restless drive.

But chariot wheels are creaking

bones begin to stir.

Before they live to haunt us and pursue

move on.

The cord is cut

the afterbirth is out.

Home is always somewhere else

along the hunted way.

Exile

Exile has its compensations,
fascinating fruit beyond old catalogues of sin.

Free to join the dance
between the errors of the ancient
and the follies of the new,
to enjoy among the tombstones of tradition
a quiet chuckle.

Geography of exile is not limited by seas
or barbed-wire ultimatums of despair.
As wide as a half-remembered promise
a voluntary exercise,
familiar, friendly grief,
as if identity depended on the certainty of pain.

Busy roads, jostled by every-growing crowds,
angry, on the endless journey from…

And yet in exile, when ready,
any direction can also be defined as
homeward.

Visions

I now have three positions for my glasses

over the top

distance

near.

They slide up and down my nose

in dizzying indecision

with a will entirely their own.

I must be developing a whole new set of muscles.

It used to be enough that I could waggle my ears

independently

and the raised eyebrow was almost a trademark.

Are these new skills for a new decade

or just the maturing of the old?

Life still has its questions.

It all depends on how you

see it

see it

see it.

Tel Aviv 11.11.90

Kayaking in Alaska

A tranquil sea,

a distant green horizon,

some unseen shore

to be gained.

Only the regular splash of oars,

the weight of water,

the half-glimpsed thrust

of companion craft,

sliding back and forth alongside,

suggest the reality of motion,

the relativity of motion,

while the far away land,

unchanging,

never closer,

mocks our dip and pull,

dip and pull,

all movement

illusory,

all effort

futile.

Like those childhood dreams

running in slow motion,

feet anchored in tar,

leaden muscles,

heart pounding

unable to reach…

to act…

to save…

In time the contours of the land shift,

our mental geography reasserts its grip,

channels define themselves,

measurable distances emerge,

details multiply,

a haven awaits.

But that timelessness,

that helpless effort

to move, advance, grasp …

how it haunts,

redefines all certainty.

To arrive

is just a moment,

a time and a place

without task or future,

like that other eternity,

death;

to journey

is to be alive,

but how distant the shoreline,

how heavy the weight of water.

Fukuoka May 2010

Postscript

On the way

> On the way from here to there,
>
> somewhere.
>
> Though not 'anywhere',
>
> for 'not anywhere'
>
> is not 'nowhere'.
>
> Wherever we are
>
> is where we are
>
> even on our way
>
> elsewhere.
>
> So, there we are!
>
> Away from 'here'
>
> not yet 'there'
>
> but aware.

28.8.01

About the author

Jonathan Magonet entertaining in Japan

Jonathan Magonet was born in London and qualified as a medical doctor before studying to become a rabbi at Leo Baeck College in London. On graduation he taught Hebrew Bible at the College, becoming its Principal from 1985-2005.

For over 40 years he has co-organised an annual Jewish-Christian Bible Week and annual Jewish-Christian-Muslim Student Conference, both in Germany. In December 1999 he was awarded the Cross of the Order of Merit of the Federal Republic of Germany (*Das Verdienstkreuz am Bande des Verdienstordens der*

Bundesrepublik Deutschland) for the "unceasing and dedicated contribution he has made to interfaith relations between Jews and Christians and to German-Jewish reconciliation".

As a writer he has produced several books on popular Bible scholarship, including '*A Rabbi Reads the Bible*' and '*A Rabbi Reads the Psalms*'; on interfaith dialogue *Talking to the Other*; his work on Jewish liturgy can be seen in *Forms of Prayer 1 Daily, Sabbath and Occasional Prayers (2008)* which he edited. He has recently turned to fiction with '*Netsuke Nation: Tales from Another Japan*'. He is editor of the journal *European Judaism* and is currently a Visiting Research Professor at Seinan Gakuin University, Fukuoka, Japan

He is married to Dorothea and they have two children, Gavriel and Avigail, a grandson Ephra and granddaughter Arava.

His website is www.jonathanmagonet.co.uk

Acknowledgments

First and foremost I want to thank my wife Dorothea not only for her lovely design for the cover of this book, but for putting up with my journeys and absences during which many of these poems were written.

I am grateful to Marc Michaels for bringing his great skills at layout and his publishing craft to the production of this book.

Lastly, I owe a great debt to the people I have met other the years who, in very different ways, with or without their knowledge, have inspired the poems that are to be found in this volume.

Other books by Jonathan Magonet

Full details and links to publications at
www.jonathanmagonet.co.uk

A Rabbi Reads the Bible
ISBN-13: 9780334029526
Jonathan Magonet
Published 2004

Rabbi Magonet's love of the Hebrew Bible developed whilst studying to be a Rabbi. Studying the Bible became a source of comfort, challenge and religious growth, without sacrificing the importance of the scientific approaches of study. This book opens up the Bible so that all readers will find their perspective and understanding changed.

A Rabbi Reads the Psalms
ISBN-13: 9780334029533
Jonathan Magonet
Published 2004

After teaching the Psalms for over twenty years, Magonet has found very little on rabbinical interpretation, ancient, mediaeval or modern.
This is an introduction to the Hebrew text that gives access to the richness and complexity of the language of the Psalms to the non-Hebrew reader.

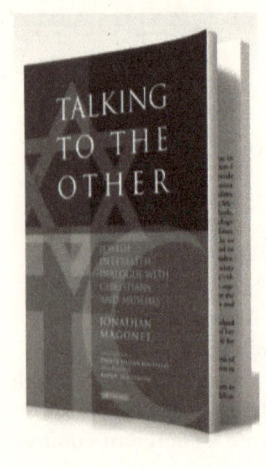

Talking to the Other
ISBN: 9781860649059
Jonathan Magonet
Published 2003

Suicide killings have focused world attention on international terrorism. The involvement of people claiming that their Islamic faith justified murderous suicide action has intensified the demonization of Islam in the West, and in turn highlighted the need to understand and relate to Muslims in all their diversity. Rabbi Jonathan Magonet has long been engaged in interfaith dialogue, and in this book he explores the issues that arise with such an encounter and challenges the Jewish community to broaden its commitment to interfaith dialogue in a complex and rapidly changing world.

Netsuke Nation
Tales from another Japan
ISBN: 9781860649059
Jonathan Magonet
Published 2003

Before Manga captured the imagination of the world, Japanese artists sculpted a miniature society of human and not-quite human characters. These are 'netsuke': tiny figures, threaded by cords, which were used to hold in place the 'purse' that hung from a kimono. Carved from wood, ivory or bone, they formed an exotic society, reflecting the history, culture and fantasy life of Japan.

Now, for the first time, their individual stories come to life, and the unfamiliar and often startling nature of their society. Meet Momo, the beautiful but conflicted geisha cat; discover the dreams of the mermaids who worship Esther Williams; witness the rise and fall of a ruthless politician who plays the 'alien' card; encounter the creatures of legend and the demons who star in horror movies; learn the peculiar practices and customs of netsuke sexuality; try to solve the mystery of why netsuke suddenly disappear; admire the heroic quest to create a national orchestra; enjoy the embarrassment of a martial arts struggle gone peculiarly awry; share the hopes of an autumn and spring love story; face the threat to netsuke society of the plastic invasion.

Forms of Prayer
Published 2008

Part of Jonathan's ongoing work has been editing prayerbooks for the Movement for Reform Judaism, most recently the 2008 'Forms of Prayer - Daily, Sabbath and occasional prayer' *Seder Ha-t'fillot*. Work is currently underway on a new edition of the High Holyday prayer book.

Jonathan Magonet, 2013.

Other books from Kulmus Publishing

Print, pdf and epub versions all available through www.lulu.com and some through other on-line booksellers.
Catalogue available at www.kulmus.co.uk

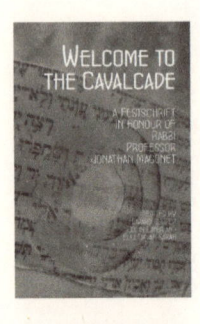

Welcome to the Cavalcade

A *Festschrift* in honour of
Rabbi Professor Jonathan Magonet
Edited by Rabbi Howard Cooper, Rabbi Colin Eimer and Rabbi Elli Tikvah Sarah
Various Contributors © 2013

A celebration by his rabbinic and academic colleagues of Rabbi Professor Jonathan Magonet's unique contribution to the Jewish and wider world.

Megillat B'ney Chashmonay (The Scroll of the Hasmonean Sons)

ISBN: 978-0-9880539-0-8
Marc Michaels © 2013

There isn't a scroll read on *Chanukah* but perhaps there should be? *Sofer STa"M* Marc Michaels has gathered over twenty handwritten and printed manuscripts from the 13th Century onwards for this traditional text for *Chanukah* that used to be read in Italian, Yemenite and other synagogues.

Examining the variant Hebrew and Aramaic texts, he has created a new *tikkun kor'im* fully pointed with vowels and trope and a new *tikkun sofrim* with visual *midrashim* to add extra depth to the text. A new translation into English with explanatory notes is accompanied by a new commentary on the text - *Or LiM'norah* in the style of the biblical commentators. Includes two 'missing' verses found in the oldest Aramaic manuscripts but expunged from later Hebrew ones.

Megillat HaY'shuah
ISBN: 978-0-9810947-9-3
Marc Michaels © 2008

The salvation scroll of the Yemenite Jews tells a parable of the dangers of the time to the Jewish population of Yemen and how Rabbi Shalom saves the day!

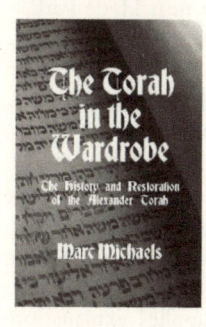

The Torah in the Wardrobe
ISBN: 978-1-988947-00-6
Marc Michaels © 2017

Written in 1790, the Alexander Torah has been passed down from generation to generation. Escaping the flames of Kristalnacht, this special Torah, full of rare scribal practices, has been rescued once more by *Sofer STa"M* (scribe) Marc Michaels (Mordechai Pinchas). He chronicles both its travels from Thälmassing to Belsize Square and its careful restoration. Jam-packed with photos.

Tam (Simple)
ISBN 978-0-9880539-7-7
Marc Michaels © 2017

PSALM 15 - KING DAVID'S GUIDE FOR THE SUCCESSFUL BUSINESS PERSON

King David has left us a person specification that we would be well served to adopt in today's business world where, sadly, ethics can be somewhat lacking. In five short verses and a mere fifty-four words the character traits that are described, show those who engage in business the appropriate way to undertake that business. Marketer and scribe, Marc Michaels follows along David's Way to unlock the business lessons for today from Psalm 15.

Restoring the Tyburn Megillah
ISBN 978-0-9810947-7-9
Marc Michaels © 2013

Jewish scribes don't often encounter Roman Catholic nuns. In a truly interfaith endeavour *Sofer STa"M* Mordechai Pinchas (Marc Michaels) chronicles the restoration of a several hundred year old manuscript of the book of Esther belonging to the nuns of the Tyburn Convent near Hyde Park.

Tikkun Megillat Hashoah
ISBN: 978-0-9810947-1-7
Marc Michaels © 2008

Authorised by the Schechter Institute and the Rabbinic Assembly, this is the *Tikkun* (copyist's guide) for the *Megillat Hashoah* (Holocaust scroll). It contains the full unpointed text in full colour hand-written *STa"M*. It also supplies explanations of the various visual *midrashim* and information about how the scroll came to be written and the importance of this new piece of liturgy.

GIVE!
ISBN: 978-0-9810947-6-2
Marc Michaels © 2009

An analysis of the biblical commandment to support the poor with particular reference to the Tannaitic interpretation in *Sifre* to *D'varim* 15:7-11. Discover how the ancient rabbis applied the *Torah* law to their own time and what lessons we might learn today about how best to ... GIVE! (169 pages with illustrations)

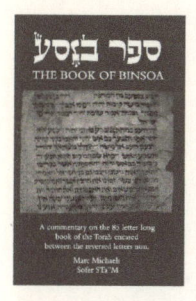

Sefer Binsoa
ISBN: 978-0-9810947-7-9
Marc Michaels © 2010

In the majority of *Torah* scrolls *Bamidbar* 10:35-36 is encased between two critical marks, each taking the form of an inverted nun. *Sofer STa"M* Marc Michaels examines this unique visual midrash and provides a commentary that explains why *Sefer Binsoa* should be considered important and what lessons it might hold for us today.

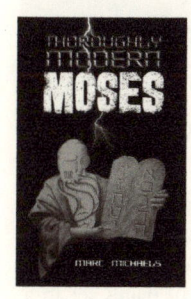

Thoroughly Modern Moses
ISBN: 978-0-9810947-4-8
Marc Michaels © 2009

Joseph Rosenberg, not so eminent Jewish scientist and time-traveller came to Earth with a bump and was surprised, nay shocked, to learn that he had landed on one of the most famous people in the history of history itself ... Moses the Lawgiver. Ordered to replace Moses by the Lord God Almighty, Supreme Being of the Universe and all round Nice-Guy, Mr. Rosenberg embarks on an adventure of biblical proportions. Will he survive? Will there be tea and cake? A science-fiction biblical comedy. Hitch-Hikers meets the Bible - enjoy! (Contains over 300 pages of laughter).

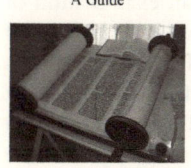

Care of Your Torah - A Guide
ISBN: 978-0-9810947-2-4
Marc Michaels © 2008

A short 19 page guide written by a *Sofer STa"M* (scribe) to help Synagogues care for their Torah scrolls. With lots of useful tips and photographs showing many examples of what can make a Torah *pasul* (not kosher).

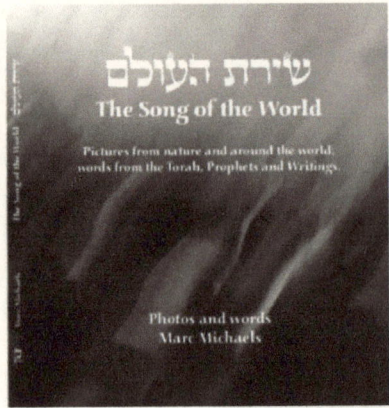

Shirat Ha-Olam - The Song of the World
ISBN: 978-0-9810947-0-0 Marc Michaels © 2009

Pictures from nature and around the world; words from the *Torah*, Prophets and Writings. Seventy digitally unaltered photographs matched to an appropriate biblical verse - each with its own story, told in this inspirational book. A feast for the eyes and the mind (149 pages set in a special *sofrut* inspired font and Palantino).

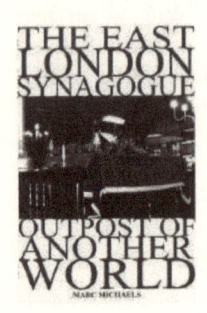

The East London Synagogue - Outpost of another World
ISBN: 978-0-9810947-3-1
Marc Michaels © 2008

A short history of the early days of the East London Synagogue, Rectory Square, and an examination of how it came to be established in 1877. Described by the Revd. Joseph Stern as 'a rallying point in this locality' what was the intended role for this 'outpost of another world'? Did it succeed? An examination of the historical documents together with rare photos taken shortly before the closure of the building, and from other sources.

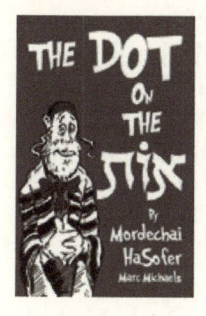

The Dot on the Ot
Marc Michaels © 2016

A tribute in the style of the wonderful 'Cat in the Hat', the 'Dot on the Ot' teaches about the famous dots on the letters that occur in the *Sefer Torah*. It has been created by Mordechai Pinchas HaSofer (aka Marc Michaels), *sofer STa"M* (scribe) for adults and children alike in loving memory of his wonderful nephew Nadav Ezra *z"l*. It is not intended for sale or profit. Download free from http://bit.ly/1PMboMK

The E-Fuzzy
ISBN: 978-0-9810947-5-5
Marc Michaels © 2017

Too much screen time can be a bad thing for everyone! Will Popplethewaite ever understand why the children playing are so happy? Will the children rescue their Warm Fuzzy from his clutches? Or will they spend too much time staring at their E-Fuzzies to care? Find out in the 'The E-FUZZY'. A sequel to the excellent 'Original Warm Fuzzy Tale' by Claude M. Steiner. Written with kind permission of the original author. A cautionary TALE FOR EVERYONE. Illustrated throughout.

Mordy Potter and the Philosopher's Bagel
Marc Michaels © 2017

A Purim *shpiel* to delight young and old, very very loosely based on the Harry Potter books and films with a healthy dose of Jewish fun thrown in for good measure. With cast and props and stage directions, a ready made playlet written by *Sofer STa"M* Marc Michaels for you to adapt for your synagogue's Purim celebrations. A free download not for sale from Kulmus Publishing. Download link: bit.ly/2kMsvzG

Festschrift for Rabbi Maurice Michaels
ISBN: 978-0-9810947-8-6
Edited by Marc Michaels © 2011
A collection of essays on Jewish themes to mark the occasion of Rabbi Maurice Michaels' 70th birthday written by rabbinical colleagues.

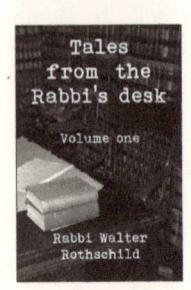

Tales from the Rabbi's Desk Vol. 1
ISBN: 978-0-9880539-2-2
Rabbi Walter Rothschild © 2015
Rabbi Walter Rothschild brings us a collection of stories, some fiction, some based on fact that give an insight into the rich tapestry of human lives that he and his colleagues have touched.

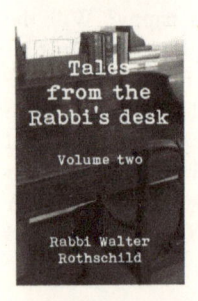

Tales from the Rabbi's Desk Vol. 2
ISBN: 978-0-9880539-5-3
Rabbi Walter Rothschild © 2016
Rabbi Walter Rothschild presents a second selection of his 'Tales', based on his own experience and those of his colleagues, all working at that invisible interface between the Human and the Divine.

Women Rabbis in the Pulpit
ISBN: 978-0-9880539-3-9
Editors: Rabbi Dr Barbara Borts & Rabbi Elli Tikvah Sarah © 2015
A collection of sermons by women rabbis dedicated to the memory of the first woman Rabbi, Regina Jonas who was ordained on December 27, 1935. Sermons cover topics under the headings Living a Jewish Life, Being Human, God and Spirituality, Responses and Responsibility to the World, Feminism and Gender and Life and Loss.